The
Referee's
Referee
BECOMING THE BEST

ABRAHAM KLEIN
RUBI SHALEV

as told to **Paul Harris**

Dedicated to

The late **ARTEMIO FRANCHI**
Formerly Vice President of FIFA
President of UEFA and
Chairman of the Referees' Committee of FIFA

With special thanks to
Yaron Friedman, artist
Hillery Greenberg and
Robert Lovy, cover design

Soccer for Americans
Box 836, Manhattan Beach, California 90266 • (310) 372-9000

מדינת ישראל
STATE OF ISRAEL
MINISTRY OF EDUCATION, CULTURE AND SPORT

Jerusalem   ירושלים
כ"ד בתשרי תשנ"ה
September 29, 1994

INTRODUCTION TO ABRAHAM KLEIN'S BOOK

The Israeli Representative Soccer Team didn't play at the World's Cup Final Tournament in Argentina (78) and in Spain (82), but the Israeli flag flew in those countries' stadiums and also in many other competitions all over the world, although Israel didn't play there, and that is to Abraham Klein's credit, the number one referee ("the man with the whistle") in Israel.

Abraham Klein became a referee at an early age and shortly became one of the senior, local and international referees for many years. He also served as Senior Referee in the Israeli League.

Abraham works to improve the occupation of refereeing and uses his vast experience to change the refereeing in Israel to professional, to advance the status of soccer, referees and contributes a lot to education and to the training of the young generation of referees.

Through Abraham Klein's enormous experience and reputation, he made friends and connections all over the world, connections which contributed a lot to the advancement and strengthening of Israeli sport and its intermingling into many international frameworks.

His vast international experience he contributes to the public authority.
This book, written in professional language opens before the experienced and young soccer referee a new world which will help him march into <u>victory in the 21st century</u>.

Congratulations!

Sincerely,

MK Micha Goldman
Deputy Minister

FROM PAUL HARRIS

My first impression of Abraham Klein was indelible, and extremely positive. The occasion brought 18,000 partisans to a closed-circuit presentation of a great event: England-Brazil at Guadalajara in 1970 at the World Cup. Klein was "in the middle". I witnessed, from 1400 miles away, an emergence of a giant among men. I still view this film when I need special inspiration.

I hope that this book provides you with insights, thoughts, and inspiration. Whether you strive for international achievement is beside the point; we want, above all, to enable you to improve, to do better in all your games. The great game of soccer will be the benefactor. We want you to live your referee life as an exclamation, not an explanation!

The theme of this book resides in "completion". Abraham began in youth games, as we all did, but he's different in two ways. First, he made it to the top, and after spending many years there, he is still giving to the game. He referees in youth leagues and tournaments, quietly setting the example for the future generations of players and referees.

Abraham once told me a story from the dressing room. An internationally known troublemaker found himself, before game time, having his equipment under close scrutiny. As Klein examined the shoe, he found himself grasping the player's wrist. "I merely applied just a little bit of pressure, ever so slight, so he knew I was making a point." Klein said, 'We'll have no problems today, will we?' " The lesson for us: There are _many_ ways to referee.

Even if you absorbed all of the information in this book, and put it to use in your games, it could work against you. The object is not to make you a clone of a respected soccer official from Israel. Our hope is that you will continue to develop your own referee personality, then think seriously about what works for others. Develop your own tactical game plan. We'd love to know how it's working for you!

Paul Harris

FROM ABRAHAM KLEIN

The main purpose of this book is to advise the referee on how to improve in two basic areas.

First, there is physical preparation: Readying your body for rigorous demands. Secondly, mental preparation: Readying your mind for any non-physical challenge on the field of play.

Without these two important areas of preparation, the referee will not be able to succeed in performing his duties, no matter how experienced he may be. The referee has to be at the peak of concentration level during the game. Even a few seconds of vagueness might influence the game, and with catastrophic results!

Everybody sees the referee in action. He is at the center of the events, often presenting an exposure that he prefers not to have! It is very important to make the most accurate and correct decisions. In order to succeed, he must be very close to the events. This can be achieved only by being physically fit.

The referee has to prepare himself physically at three different levels:

1. Before the season.
2. During the season.
3. Before refereeing in specific games.

Serious physical fitness preparation can be achieved by knowing the physical activities which are executed by the referee during the game:

1. Running for about 15 km. at a medium pace.
2. Short and long sprints.
3. The changing of speed and direction while running.
4. Physical and mental reactions.
5. Running backwards.
6. Side running.
7. Avoiding the path of the ball or unpredictable movements of players.

The mental preparation includes a variety of topics: How you feel about yourself, the game, the players, other officials, and how the Laws can work for you. *The Referee's Referee* contains thoughts and ideas for any and all referees and linesmen in the great game of soccer. My personal hope is that you will continue your commitment to refereeing, always passing on your knowledge to others.

The
Referee's Referee
BECOMING THE BEST

TABLE OF CONTENTS

SPECIAL WORDS FROM PELÉ

My good friend Joseph Blatter, FIFA's General Secretary, in his "FIFA NEWS" editorial - "Judgement in Favor of Positive Football" - properly defined the great importance and responsibility of the Referees and Linesmen in encouraging attacking play; implementing the Laws of the Game more positively in line with the decisions made by the International Football Association Board; and "shielding the creative genius on the field more effectively from technically inferior opponents who delve in dirty tricks to stop him".

Those who followed my career on the playing fields of the world know very well that I faced a lot of good and honest defenders, but also those who used violent plays to stop me. I always worked hard to force the International Board and the Referee Associations to stop those dirty tricks that were destroying the artistry and the happiness of our beautiful game!

Finally, we could see some of the enforcement of the Laws during World Cup USA 1994. This made most of the 52 games played in the American territory more open and more offensive which attracted record crowds in the stadia and more TV coverage in the USA and worldwide.

I met Abraham Klein in WC Mexico 1970, when he refereed Brazil versus England, a game that I considered the most important on the way to the third Brazil World Cup championship. It was a tough game but he always had total control of the action.

His international referee career was always praised by his peers, coaches and players. Now, he is one of the referee instructors running clinics and courses all over the world and he has decided to write this book which arrives at just the right time.

Those who love our beautiful game, I am sure, will be pleased with this authentic referee textbook in which Abraham has put all his experience and his theoretical and practical knowledge in a meticulous and well-researched work.

Congratulations, Abraham, for a job well done!

Your friend and admirer from Brazil,

Pelé and Abraham Klein have met many times, but the most dramatic meeting was in Guadalajara, Mexico, June 7, 1970.

22 International "A" Games
Refereed by Abraham Klein

Year	Teams	Score
1964	Holland - Israel	1-0
1965	Italy - Poland	0-1
1968	Spain - Brazil	1-0
1968	Japan - Mexico	2-0
1970	Brazil - England	1-0
1972	Paraguay - Peru	1-0
1972	Yugoslavia - Paraguay	2-1
1972	Yugoslavia - Bolivia	1-1
1972	Russia - Uruguay	1-0
1972	Brazil - Scotland	1-0
1972	Brazil - Portugal	1-0
1976	Poland - Cuba	0-0
1976	Russia - Brazil	2-0
1976	Italy - England	2-0
1978	Italy - Argentina	1-0
1978	Austria - West Germany	3-2
1978	Brazil - Italy	2-1
1979	Rest of the World - Argentina	2-1
1979	Austria - Hungary	3-1
1980	Italy - Yugoslavia	2-0
1982	Italy - Brazil	3-2
1983	Italy - Yugoslavia	2-2

THE CHARACTER OF THE REFEREE

T hough many choose to referee the sport that sometimes holds the world in its grip, not all officials continue their dedication. Many fall short of their goals of excellence and recognition. In their desire for acknowledgement and satisfaction, many fail to examine the qualities that will serve them in any of life's challenges.

Examine carefully the virtues, or character traits, and ask yourself how you would find examples from your own experience, stories, or anecdotes that center on your personality.

PERSEVERANCE

Most referees begin and end their careers in the narrow frame of one or two years. Klein began whistling at the age of 22, first with youth games, then adults through semi-professionals and professionals. The First League of Israel (16 teams) and a variety of assignments in Greece toughened him up for World Cup and Olympics qualifying games. Always his own greatest critic, he wondered after each game and incident: "Could I have done better?" He never abandoned the dream of major international competition at the World Cup Finals.

COMPASSION

Whether it's the World Cup or a meaningless game late in the season, Abraham Klein prepares the same. From the opening whistle, you have to feel the tackle, and know what it's like to experience the sting of defeat and disappointment. The referee who has compassion for players loves the game, and protects players by an equal application of the Laws.

SELF DISCIPLINE

A soccer game makes high demands on all who participate. Preparation consists of both physical and mental dedication. The 1994 World Cup referees were monitored by FIFA medical personnel for a year prior to the tournament, under conditions that simulated the expected oppressive conditions in the nine venues. Klein, more than twenty years earlier, self-imposed these rigorous tests, and was considered among the most fit of all referees in World Cup history.

COURAGE

It is helpful for referees to face the reality of their appointment. Klein often told other referees, "I know I have no friends out there. I am not afraid of any crowd, of any player, of any coach." The great Pelé recognized Klein's superior performance in the Brazil-England classic during the 1970 World Cup. "I met Abraham Klein in WC Mexico 1970 when he refereed Brazil vs. England, a game that I consider the most important on the way to the third Brazil World Cup Championship. It was a tough game, but he always had total control of the action." The partisan crowd wanted a penalty kick when Pele went down in the first half. It takes courage to call fouls, and equal courage not to call them.

LOYALTY

No matter the circumstance, Klein elevates, supports, and values fellow officials. He still learns from the experience of others, and is anxious to share his own wisdom. He is loyal to the game, and to those both above and below him in authority.

FAIRNESS

A soccer parent once said, "The trouble with referees is that they don't care who wins." A sense of fairness must be paramount with each move, with each tackle, each judgement on the field of play. Here, Klein is a natural extension of his personality, and proof that there is room for gentlemen in the refereeing "profession". Generations of players have saluted this quality.

RESPECT

Klein knows that whatever you do in refereeing, you are tilling the ground for those who follow. Respect for other referees means a deep understanding of problems that can occur, and a willing search for ways to make the paths easier. His authority breathes respect for and from players.

What Others Are Saying...

"He is not frightened to make unpopular decisions if he is convinced that they are the right ones."

Norman Giller, London Daily Express

BECOMING A REFEREE'S REFEREE

The 1994 World Cup brought a new awareness to the game. The quality performances of all promise to bring new coaches, spectators, and referees to soccer. Spectators are responding to an increasingly attractive game that brings excitement and emotion. Coaches will expect more of players, and everyone anticipates higher performances from those who are to control all levels of play. As you proceed on your way in officiating, there are a few things that will help you to become a **REFEREE'S REFEREE.**

1. Ask an experienced referee to evaluate you. While it is true that few know what to look for, the exercise in assessment will aid you both.
2. Study the "experienced" referees who are above you. Find those admirable qualities and habits that fit your own personality, and try them in games.
3. Listen intently to coaches on the sideline when others are in the middle.
4. Take an interest outside of reffing. Read books by coaches, and on the game in general.
5. Go to some games to watch play, not referees. In the interest of "ref watching", too many referees forget about the game itself.

Joseph "Sepp" Blatter, General Secretary of FIFA, has had a long and positive influence on the development of referees. He has also been a strong advocate of law changes that provide attractive soccer and limit negative play.

6. Try something new each game. It may be only a gesture, a new technique, or a method of running, but it may keep you more alert.

7. Write an "attitude" test for yourself, take the test, and have another referee look at it.

8. Keep a record of all your games, a "journal", including cautions, ejections, scores, etc. Are you officiating too much? Too many problems?

9. Take on at least one administrative position. If you can't lecture, recruit. If you can't recruit, volunteer to grade examinations. Write a newsletter. Show a movie. Do something!

10. Play a little soccer. Know what it's like to be tripped or shoulder-charged.

The future of the game resides with the new generation of referees, players, and coaches. The youngest of players at the Dallas Cup receives compliments from Bill Stroube, Executive Director of the competition. Many people work industriously to pave the way for the future of "the beautiful game". Stanley Lover (at left, with hat), and Tom Wharton, to his left, have encouraged referees in a variety of ways.

THE REFEREE'S CODE OF CONDUCT

"Perfection is the duty, not the goal, of the referee"

At the Dallas Cup, a substitution comes in. Prepare for everything, no matter what the level of play.

DO BE...
- Available when needed.
- Empathetic.
- Supportive.
- Calm.
- Thinking, preparing for everything.
- Consistent.
- Confident.
- Ready, alert.

DON'T BE...
- Argumentative.
- Critical.
- Abusive.
- Over-reactive.
- Losing temper or control.
- Refereeing to please anyone.
- Influenced by anyone.
- Complacent, lethargic.

10 TEN COMMANDMENTS FOR SOCCER REFEREES

1. TRY TO TRAIN TWICE A WEEK.
2. TRY TO WORK ON SPEED TWICE A WEEK.
3. YOU MUST WORK ON FLEXIBILITY EVERYDAY.
4. STRENGTH TRAINING - 2-3 TIMES A WEEK.
5. ENDURANCE TRAINING - "DAILY BREAD".
6. PROTECT YOUR BACK - DO NOT RUN ON PAVED ROADS, RUN ON SOFT SURFACES, GRASS AND TIGHT SAND.
7. TAKE CARE OF YOUR LIQUID BALANCE - YOU MUST DRINK AT LEAST 4 LITERS OF LIQUID EACH TRAINING DAY.
8. EAT CARBOHYDRATES BEFORE THE GAME.
9. GOOD WARM-UPS IS A REQUIREMENT, EVEN BEFORE THE GAME!
10. AT THE COMPLETION OF INTENSIVE EFFORTS, YOU MUST PERFORM RECOVER EXERCISES. (COOL-DOWN EXERCISES).

THE GREATEST GAME...
A REFEREE'S TRIUMPH

"It had been a magnificent, enthralling display of football,
admirably refereed by the obscure Israeli referee,
Abraham Klein: an inspired appointment"
Brian Glanville - History of the World Cup

Some soccer historians call it the greatest game ever played. The setting on June 7, 1970 could not have been better... the defending World Cup champions, England, facing probably the most skillful Brazilian team ever assembled. Though FIFA's "Year of the Referee" was still 16 years in the future, this occasion could now be called "The Referee's Triumph".

It's only a cramp, and Klein makes sure that the trainer doesn't come on the field. Pelé, the great sportsman that he is, helps with the problem.

Abraham Klein, 36, and with 6 internationals under his belt, and now facing his greatest challenge, was in full control. The climatic atmosphere at Jalisco Stadium in Guadalajara in Mexico favored Brazil, AND Klein! He was ready for the 100 degree temperature and the 6500 foot altitude, as he had trained for 21 days at even higher altitudes.

The game was not 30 seconds old when Klein met a minor challenge to his athleticism. As a through-ball passed midfield, a sprinting Klein, without losing a step, turned and at medium speed ran backwards for a full 10 yards. A close observer would immediately know that this World Cup game was being controlled with full authority. Almost two hours later, everyone in attendance reflected that the simplest game had been showcased at its best, and that all had contributed to the enjoyment. Shirts were exchanged with eleven different conversations taking place among great sportsmen. No one wanted to leave the field. It was the "Final before the Final".

WHAT REALLY HAPPENED TO THE PLAYERS

- Gordon Banks' save from Pelé's header is now considered the greatest save in World Cup history.
- Only one yellow card was shown.
- There were no injuries, displays of bad temper, or ill feelings.
- Only 29 fouls were whistled, two of them for hand balls. In the first half, England went 16 minutes without a foul, and in the second half, 19 minutes passed with no English infractions.
- Pelé had only 77 touches of the ball, but completed 22 of 29 passes, and committed only one foul. Fouled only once, Pelé's brilliant and unselfish pass led to the game's only goal.
- In the 1970 World Cup, not one player was sent off the field of play!
- The game was called Bobby Moore's greatest. As captain of his team, he committed no fouls, and proved that the game can be played almost to perfection. A tower of strength and skill, with 104 ball touches in the game, Moore successfully completed 36 of 40 passes!

A REFEREE... IN CONTROL

- The game contained 75 incidents of contact where "50/50 balls" could have resulted in "50/50 fouls". The advantage was used liberally.
- No situations emerged where Klein was out of position to call an apparent infraction.
- Two appeals for penalty kicks were both ignored. "Not calling the penalty for Pelé was the best decision of my life", Klein would say years later.
- Klein did not impose himself on free kicks. Players did not challenge authority through encroachment. With only one exception, free kicks were taken without time wasting.
- In a manner that was to serve as a model for future competitions, Klein pressured both trainers and players to leave the field quickly when "injuries" were in evidence. He was years ahead of his time in this aspect of control.

Klein's performance reflected a great sensitivity for the occasion. Pelé himself said after the 1966 World Cup that it would be his last, but in Mexico, he was protected by the referee and respected by the English. (He had been brutally fouled in 1966.) Klein knew both teams well: nowhere on the field would players be given extra space for unchallenged possession. Pressure soccer brought little chance for rest, and the game would go end to end with few intervals for buildup. A Brazil win of 1-0 in a game that could have been 4-3 brought positive attacking soccer back to the World Cup, and it established Klein as a model for fitness, game control, and fairness. It was a mighty performance that matched soccer's most favored occasion.

England-Brazil, early in the game. Pele's vertical jump here is at least two feet high. The opponent (hidden), knows he's beaten. Sometimes players back into a rival while he is in the air. Such a foul is dangerous, and should be called for tripping. If you are close to play you can often see the players' eyes. This gives away the intention. This photo also reveals lots of space around the challenge for the ball, making all decisions easier. Klein's position is perfect to judge all activity.

PREPARING FOR AND DELIVERING AT THE WORLD CUP '94

Mario van der Ende

In World Cup '94, the 24 FIFA referees proved they could meet the physical challenges of heat, humidity, and end to end play. Specific training had begun almost a year prior to the games for Mario van der Ende of Holland.

Under the care of a doctor of physiology, the 38 year old teacher of sociology from Den Haag used the same physical program as the world famous Ajax Club, with three of Holland's most noted triathletes and the national men's field hockey team! With a five day a week training program (75 minutes), he also reported for biweekly medical checkups. Weight, blood pressure and heart performance were all carefully monitored.

During this time of intensive preparation for the most demanding World Cup ever, van der Ende engaged in sprinting and interval training, coupled with a regular match in Holland's first division.

Indoor training was conducted in extreme heat, and the last week included exposure to saunas, with three T-shirts and a plastic overall for a realistic preview of the game sites. Most of the training was with World Cup Linesman Jan Dolstra, with emphasis on teamwork and mental preparation. Evert Wyers, National Referee trainer, supervised it all. With even the power and strength of his leg muscles under the scrutiny of Dutch and FIFA officials, van der Ende was ready for the World Cup that would bring out the best in the world's best.

"During my three matches (Ireland-Italy in New York, USA-Romania in Los Angeles, and Switzerland-Spain in Washington) I never had problems with the weather. The preparation was perfect for the occasion."

Following three successful games at WC '94, Mario relaxes with a beach workout at Haifa, Israel with Abraham and Amit Klein.

FIFA's LAWS

MAKING THEM WORK FOR YOU

"The laws of the game are a monument to all of those who have played the game in the past."
Sir Stanley Rous, "Football Worlds"

Many officials once played soccer, but their first exposure to the Laws of the Game was probably a few weeks before their first referee experience. Written for those who officiate in almost 200 countries, they have undergone a slow transformation in almost 150 years of play. Almost anyone can take a FIFA book and pass an examination on the 17 Laws, but that is not enough. A keen knowledge of the game is just as important as familiarity. Those who grow to love the game must stress the "why" of these Laws. Many referees use the Laws only as a guideline, "prescriptions for fair play", even "standards for enjoyment" of all who participate. Referees are also encouraged to read the International Board Decisions, which guide referees on how to make decisions.

Sir Stanley Rous of England wrote the modern Laws of the Game. Long before his days as President of FIFA, he poses here at St. James Park, in 1934. Rous also invented the Diagonal System of Control in that year. He was known for his devotion to sportsmanship, and was never at a loss for words: "The only way to satisfy the craving for immediate achievement is to change the laws so that BOTH sides win."

HINTS AND IDEAS ABOUT THE LAWS

Law I The Field of Play
- Pre-game inspection of the field, including goal posts, nets (not required), corner flags, and bench areas is vital for safety and uniformity.

> *Idea:* The line between the goalposts is the most important one on the field. Make sure this line is accurately placed.

"The lines belong to the areas of which they are the boundaries." Does it surprise you that these words are in Law IX? If so, read the Laws again.

Law II The Ball
- Occasionally your authority may be challenged by the visiting team in the selection of the game ball.

> *Idea:* Be in charge of the game ball from your first inspection until game's end. If the game ball is not returned to you at game's conclusion, do not ask for it.

Law III Number of Players
- All players have equal rights, and must be treated with equal respect. Be aware of age groupings for youth soccer.

> *Idea:* Confusions about the number of players on the field can occur after halftime, when changes are made. Referee and linesmen should both count the number of players at the beginning of each period.

Law IV Players' Equipment

- Always take notice of players' equipment during a match. Look for loose shoelaces, displaced shinguards, or anything that can be dangerous to another player.

> *Idea:* Equipment problems should be addressed BEFORE the game, with time to correct the situation.

Why is this a very unusual photo? Because players seldom pose between referees and linesmen. This picture was taken just minutes before the 1982 World Cup Final. Christov of Czechoslovakia is on the left, referee Arnando Coehlo in the middle, and Abraham Klein on the right. Klein had been nominated to referee the Final, should it have to be replayed. Italy defeated Germany, 3-1 in the Final, and a replay was not required.

Law V Referees

> *"We have to convince referees that they should*
> *be part of the spectacle of soccer."*
> Joseph "Sepp" Blatter, FIFA General Secretary
> from " The Simplest Game", by Paul Gardner

- The referee must bring himself just above the level of the players... close enough to experience what they are experiencing, and far enough so you're untouchable in matters of dispute. Be polite and modest.
- Do not steal anyone's performance. Even referees who have limited ambitions in the game should also constantly strive for improvement.
- Every player must, in some way, understand who is the referee.
- Referees should be more concerned about what players do than by what they say.
- Do your thinking in clinics, at halftime, before and after the game. Resist the temptation to ponder your decisions. Through your experience, you must learn to REACT! DECIDE, DON'T DEBATE!

Idea: Consider the amount of preparation required to place a team on the field. The referee's preparation should be no less exhaustive.

Referees should always look and be more disciplined than the players. On Abraham Klein's left is Michel Zen-Ruffinen, a FIFA referee from Switzerland, and Assistant to the General Secretary of FIFA.

The referee will have to make only three or four major decisions in an average match. Are you physically and mentally prepared for these decisions?

Law VI Linesmen

"Arrayed against us are both teams, players, coaches, and most fans. It is just about even, as long as we stay together."

- A linesman is there to assist the referee, not to manage a game.
- Linesmen are always closer to spectators and to the substitutes. It is therefore the linesman's duty to report all activity that may negatively affect the game.
- Dissent against linesmen is to be treated the same as dissent against the referee.
- Linesmen should be ready for anything. Abraham Klein was on the line in June of 1970 when Pelé, upon seeing the Czechoslovakian goalkeeper standing on his "18 yard line", took a shot from midfield. The attempt surprised everyone, and missed only by inches. It would have been the most spectacular goal in World Cup history!
- In the pre-game instructions to linesmen, it is suggested that the referee may fully involve a linesmen in game preparation by asking, for example: "How do you handle free kicks near the penalty area?" .

Idea: Try to establish full eye contact with each linesman early in the game. For this to be fully effective, you must be within 20 yards of the linesman. This gesture forms a cooperative bond.

Law VII Duration of the Game
- Be aware of game duration variables in youth competitions.
- Time lost through injury incidents should be added in full to the playing time.
- In the interest of preserving the score, some players waste time, others consume it. Time consumption, such as "aimless" backpassing is legal. Time wasting, when no player has a chance for possession of the ball, may be a cautionable offense. Example: Goalkeepers sometimes waste time by delaying goal kicks or holding the ball for an unreasonable time.

Idea: After a long stoppage in play, such as for an injury, remember to blow the whistle before restarting play.

Law VIII The Start of Play
- Arrive early to your game, and start exactly on time.

Idea: After a goal, avoid the delay of the kickoff because of paperwork. Discourage excessive celebrations for goals scored.

One team is entering the playing area in a spirit of unison, by clapping. An opposing player is appearing somber, and is no doubt affected by the chanting and clapping. The third team appears ready to meet the challenge of varying expectations.

The referee and his linesmen are always a team.

Law IX Ball In and Out of Play
- Perfect positioning is essential for determining balls in and out of play. In most cases this is the linesman's responsibility.

> *Idea:* A ball that is in play discourages dissent. Always keep the game moving.

Law X Method of Scoring
- Before awarding a goal, always consult the linesman.
- The intensity of the game increases as the ball approaches the goal. Where will you be at these times?

> *Idea:* Referees should assume the final responsibility for all goal line decisions.

Law XI Off-Side

- The majority of the Linesman's attention should be on the "area of activity" where an offside position may occur, with equal attention on the second-to-last defender.
- In many off-side situations, it is recommended that the linesman wait a split second to be sure the player in off-side position is involved with play or seeking to gain an advantage.

> *Idea:* Immediately following your whilstling of an offside position, do not keep your eyes on the linesman. Play may proceed toward goal. You may need to whistle a second time.

On the diagonal, as Johann Cruyff enters the penalty area. Note also the concentration of the trailing linesman.

Law XII Fouls and Misconduct

*"There is a decline, finally,
in the tactics of intimidation."*

- When player "congestion" occurs, fouls are very likely to happen. Be close to play. Many good referees can often predict a foul.
- The referee establishes dangerous play ("Is this a ball for heading or for kicking?"). Whistle only if a dangerous situation is created.
- For cautions, first offer words to the player who was offended.
- Fouls: The vital few, the trivial many. Review once more the wisdom set forth in Law V, IBD 8.

- Which are your favorite fouls? "To someone with a hammer in his hand, everything starts looking like a nail." If you set out to look for something in your game, you WILL find it.
- Many defenders thrive on contact. Many attackers commit "non-violent" fouls as they seek to deceive defenders.
- "The showing of the yellow card seems to quiet other players as well as the offender himself..." Ken Aston "Soccer Match Control" by Stanley Lover, p 190.
- Players do not get sent off. They send themselves off.
- The lateral (side) tackle, when there is no contact with the ball, but with the opponent, should bring a caution (yellow card).
- The violent tackle from behind, with little or no attempt to play the ball, should bring a "sending off" (red card).
- The message to cheating defenders is clear: Whoever you are, wherever you cheat, you're going off. Read IBD 15, 16.

Idea: There are two common reasons for fouls leading to misconduct: (1) Lack of referee authority, and (2) Improper field positioning of the referee.

Law XIII Free-Kick
- There is no such thing as an automatic "ceremonial" free-kick.
- Do not turn your back on free-kicks. A ball could be moved, it may not travel its circumference before being played again, encroachment could occur, or you could be inadvertently struck by the ball.

Idea: All doubt is removed if you whistle for fouls and simultaneously point the direction of the kick.

An immaculate tackle from behind, or or is it? Thanks to FIFA's new law interpretation of the tackle from behind, the game is becoming more attractive to spectators and safer for players.

Offside decisions near goal are difficult. If Pelé's teammate (right) had played the ball, would Pelé be judged offside?

Law XIV Penalty-Kick

- Don't whistle for a penalty-kick if you THINK, but only if you KNOW. Penalty-kick disputes are often gamesmanship, to distract the kicker as he mentally prepares for the kick. See also the section on penalty-kick, on page 47.

> *Idea:* Good positioning and peripheral vision will enable you to judge movement of both the goalkeeper and the penalty kicker, as well as coverage for encroachment.

Under the leadership of Dr. João Havelange, President of FIFA, soccer continues to thrive throughout the sporting world.

The kicker is two steps away from the ball. Because of the infraction by the goalkeeper, do you stop play now, or await the result of the penalty kick?

Encroachment. Do you await the outcome of the kick, and caution later, or whistle now for the infringement?

Law XV Throw-In

- The player entitled to the throw-in will go after the ball more earnestly. Quick signals by flag, and sometimes words for emphasis, should eliminate these minor challenges.
- Referees and linesmen should carefully monitor possible problems on the touchline. Many ugly incidents have transpired when an opponent ventures into the unfriendly territory of the bench or supporters in pursuit of a ball.

Idea: Always assume responsibility for throw-in decisions when the touchline is close to your diagonal.

The throw-in should be a simple affair, but sometimes there are problems you didn't anticipate.

Law XVI Goal-Kick

- After awarding a goal-kick, do not turn your back on goal area activity. Walk or run backwards.
- Corner-kick and goal-kick decisions are often inaccurate. Why? Because of:
  1. The speed of the ball from a shot on goal.
  2. The congestion of players.
  3. The speed of the attack on goal.
  4. The referee and linesmen's position being far from goal.

5. The referee and linesmen's attention on foul recognition, and not on the player last touching the ball.
6. Noise factors. Commotion of players and crowd noise can often obliterate the noise of a ball being touched.
7. Fear of making a wrong decision, leading to a corner kick.

Remedies: Concentration. Watch for deflections and player reaction.

Idea: If in ANY doubt on goal line decisions, wait for the ball retrieval actions of the players. If still in doubt, award a goal-kick.

Law XVII Corner-Kick
• On the referee's diagonal, watch for encroachment on a corner-kick.

Idea: Corner kicks bring either goal attempts or counterattacks. Be alert!

XVIII The Unwritten Law of Soccer... Common Sense
• This law does not appear in the FIFA Laws of the Game, but is nevertheless the subject of discussion where referees meet. "A referee who does not possess common sense cannot make use of the other laws, for they will not help him." Abraham Klein.

Refereeing Takes Many Forms
Early in Abraham Klein's career, and following the highly successful 1970 World Cup, he was assigned to the prestigious Mini-Copa in Brazil. The tournament was to celebrate Brazil's 150 year history. Midway in the tournament, a certain game was marred by violence and red cards, a black mark on soccer and on the celebration. Organizers pondered what would happen when the final games were contested. Klein took it upon himself to meet privately and informally with the coaches of the teams he would referee. "We are all here to bring happiness to the Brazilian people. I won't allow players to act violently in my game." The coaches, players, and the referee all made an effort on behalf of the people and the game itself. The game was "peaceful", and it is one of Klein's happiest memories.

THE NORTH AMERICAN SOCCER LEAGUE

"My best schooling in life"

Klein's performance in two World Cups had caught the attention of Eddie Pearson, Director of Officials for the NASL. FIFA gave Pearson permission to approach Klein, knowing that the American experience would sharpen him even more for international assignments. He was immediately appointed to games, and whistled more than 50 in four years.

"Each team had nine or ten different mentalities (nationalities), and each expected the officiating to be the same that they were used to in their own countries," Klein observed. His game tactics had to be more vigilant than ever. Many players were at the end of their careers. Because their skills were not as sharp, they (and league officials) expected special protection.

> **"The experience taught me a lesson I never forgot. You are handling more than a game, but a collection of individuals who see tackles and challenges in different ways. I learned to study players, their tactics, and their temperaments. It's a lesson I try to pass along to all referees."**

"Six mouths agape, all wondering what's next. You can believe that Gordon Banks, right, the famous England 'keeper', isn't pointing for a penalty. That's right, it's an indirect free kick for Fort Lauderdale. At the time, we were probably the only referees in the world who had numbers on their uniforms. Everyone knew who we were."

Warm - ups
BEFORE THE GAME

1 30 light bounces.

2 10 knee lifts.

3 10 heel lifts to the backside.

4 10 hand lifts to the sides and then lower them to the side (with light bounces).

5 10 jumps crossing legs (left to right and right to left (10 x 2).

6 10 sideways bends (hands on waist - to right and left).

7   10 jumps while knees are raised towards the chest.

8   Lie down on the belly - hands forward. Legs stretched backwards. Ten back extensions - a few seconds each and relaxation.

9   10 arm circles forward and 10 backwards.

10   Hands to the back of the neck, with legs astride, left and right turns. (Ten to each side)

11   Right and left side runs in the room - 1/2 minute (slow run - not too energetic.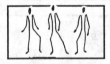

MEASURE PULSE AFTER A SERIES OF THOSE EXERCISES. 110-115 HEART BEATS PER MINUTE ARE RECOMMENDED.
After completing a series of those exercises and measuring the pulse, perform a few relaxing exercises by shaking the muscles which you have been working on (legs, back, buttock).

What Others Are Saying...

"Argentina now found themselves confronted not only by opposition as compact as a lighthouse in defense, but by referee Abraham Klein of Israel, who was unwaveringly insistent on apply the Laws of the Game, as they are written... with a resultant hail of abuse from the home country, when they lost, and widespread acclaim in Europe. Ironically, his brave conspicuous performance robbed Klein of his rightful claim to the Final."   David Miller, "The Argentina Story"

The following are flexibility exercises for stimulating important joints in your body. Perform each exercise a number of times according to the following order:

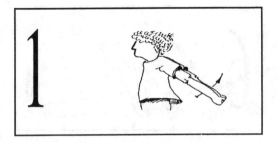

1. **Upper back, shoulders**

2. **Lower back, waist**

3. **Feet**

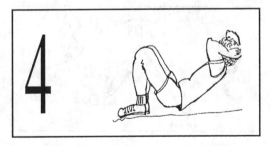

4. **Back Torso**

5. **Groins**

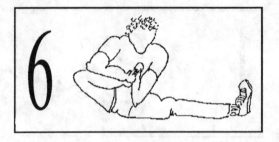

6. Legs, ankles

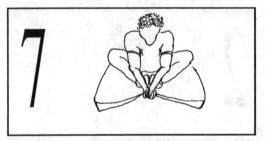

7. Groins

8. Hurdle sitting

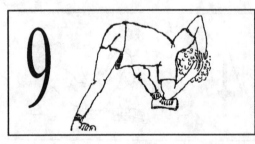

9. Back Torso feet

10. Waist

REFEREEING YOUNG PLAYERS

"A referee, no matter what his experience, should not
officiate more than one game in a day.
It is not fair to himself, the other referees, or to the teams."
Abraham Klein

A ll referees begin their avocation with young players, and many have played the game in their youth. "Soccer isn't for you", Klein's coach told him more than forty years ago. It was the culmination of several years on the bench, and a bitter disappointment. He soon decided to start anew.

It was a move from the bench to the middle of the field. "From the beginning, I always have enjoyed helping the youth, probably because I remember my 'playing' days so well. For the young, soccer is a sport without violence. Most fouls are caused by a lack of knowledge or experience and are strictly accidental." Usually the red and yellow cards are left at home. His eight years in youth soccer refereeing were helpful to him as he prepared for what awaited him in some of the most well-known stadia in the world.

FIFA encourages their referees and linesmen to take an active, strong interest in youth soccer. Look at all of the referee patches! One benefit of refereeing at the Dallas Cup is the meeting of referees, coaches, and players from so many countries.

"To children, each game is as important as the finals of the Olympics or the World Cup, and the referee must prepare and behave accordingly." said Klein at the 1994 World Cup, where he observed many players whom he had whistled in their youth. Years after he was established as a full international referee, Klein was contacted by the organizers of the Dallas Cup in Texas. This intense international competition for young boys and girls is now known throughout the soccer world, and Klein has officiated in 15 of the 16 tournaments. "I prepare for these games just as if I were reffing Brazil-England", he states. "The players expect it, and I am extremely proud to be part of this keen competition."

Is it unusual to first be seen in the final game of the World Cup, and the next year to be in the middle of a youth tournament in Scandinavia or Texas? Not for Abraham Klein. He knows that youth players and their coaches are central to the game in the 21st century. As for his home country, he officiates every Saturday in Israel, in the youth leagues, encouraging both players and a new generation of youth arbiters.

This is the best view for determining fair or unfair charging. Is this a fair shoulder charge? A push? Games with young players introduce special challenges. All referees should whistle youth soccer, whenever possible.

UNDERSTANDING THE GAME

*Referees who do not understand tactics
are powerless to deal with player deception.*

During the final raging moments of the World Cup '94 game between Belgium and Germany, Preud'homme of Belgium sprinted into the penalty area when his team was awarded a corner-kick. Unusual? Yes, for he was the Belgian goalkeeper! This move reflected the thinking of the modern game... attacking soccer, unpredictable play, and opportunistic moves that sometimes startle the imagination. The referee must be ready to deal with any tactic that occurs.

Your tactics are what you think and do on the field that surpass a mere knowledge of the laws. Some might call them survival techniques. An exemplary tactic would be Klein's entrance, after halftime, onto the field in Argentina's

Here's a restart in a game of 14-year-old players. A throw-in is being taken, yet there is no one within 15 yards. The chance of this throw-in being successful is very unlikely. Why? Where should the referee be? Is it possible this was not a legal throw-in?

national stadium in Buenos Aires. This all-important 1978 World Cup game pitting Italy against Argentina had produced a first half penalty area incident. Klein did not award a penalty kick, in spite of 80,000 protests. Emerging from the tunnel after halftime, he chose to return alongside the home team. Of course, the crowd was divided in their emotions: To verbally assault the referee, or to cheer the home team in their "must win" situation? A small point? Not at the time, and not today. Klein's thoughtful actions brought distraction, a moment of accord, and a smooth opening to a highly charged second half. "Players must always know who the referee is", is a hallmark of Klein's career.

Though the referee's actions depend largely on factors of physical and mental conditioning, his understanding of the teams and of the game itself is paramount to success. The fate of each game depends on your performance. That performance is based on what you see, and how you react. A final ingredient is the unpredictable. All the coaching talk of skills, fitness, and tactics can be shattered by one aimless swing of the foot, a ball spinning into an unwanted place, or another breaking past a post. That's what makes each game different, and perhaps is why you referee. The constant change of possession, the struggle over dominance that may change between 200 and 600 times a game. When to stop it all, and how to stop it? When to inform a player or a team, "That's enough!" The task is a mighty one, no less in a game of beginners than with struggles between nationalistic passions and pride. Advice? Look beneath the surface of every move before you make your decision, and move on! Advice? Each time the ball is turned over or a goal awarded, someone made a mistake. Your first tactic: *MAKE SURE IT IS NOT YOU WHO MADE THAT MISTAKE!*

Abraham Klein's immaculate fitness keeps him close to play, for there is no substitute for your presence when the inevitable confrontations occur. Let us look at the basic elements of the game, and at questions you should be continually asking yourself.
INDIVIDUALS

"There are fouls and there are FOULS!" Know the difference! Who are the dribblers, the ones who attack and confound the defense? Anyone can dribble in space. Who dribbles in very limited space, bringing on fouls and tackles?

Who are the tacklers, the ones who are likely to commit fouls?

Who are the team leaders, and how do they use this responsibility?

Where are the weak players?

Which skills are dominant with each player? Each player has a weakness.

How aggressive are the defenders, and the goalkeeper?

TEAM PLAY

Teams reflect the attitude, the demeanor,
and preparation of the coach.

Do players appear to prefer the advantage, or a play stoppage?

How does the defense handle the offside? Do they use the offside trap, or fall back to protect the defensive third of the field?

Is there organization, or "chance" on restarts?

Are free kicks handled quickly?

Is ball possession, with close passing, paramount, or do they rely on long passes, giving up possession for territory?

Do they mark man-to-man, or is there a zone defense?

There is little team organization here. What is likely to happen if a soft, high shot on goal were to reach these defenders in white? The ball appears to be about 20 yards from goal. What is the best position for the linesman and for the referee?

DISCIPLINE

Players and teams lacking discipline present
an immediate problem to the referee.

Do the players let small things bother them, like the awarding of a throw-in?

Do they show dissent by word or action?

How do players communicate with each other?

Do they support one another, or are they easily discouraged and fragmented?

How do they respond to instructions from the bench?

NEGATIVE TACTICS

Players instinctively know what is right or wrong,
though they may not know the Laws of the Game.

Are fouls clearly against the spirit of the game, or are they incidental?

Are skillful players being shut down? How do the react to this?

Is physical intimidation part of play?

Are fouls with the whole body (charging, jumping at) and therefore more easily seen, or more subtle, such as the holding, pushing, or tripping infractions?

ANY play involving the goalkeeper is critical!

Abraham Klein with Pelé and with Sandor Puhl from Hungary in Budapest following the World Cup '94. Puhl referred the final game in Los Angeles.

SOME WAYS IN WHICH PLAYERS CHALLENGE REFEREES

*The crowd can influence players, and players
can influence the referee.*

Swim in oceans, but remember not to sink in streams.

When you are challenged, deal with it immediately. Here are some ways in which referees are being challenged, and how you can help yourself.

The direct verbal challenges during play.
"Whose kick ref?" "Our ball?" If you get involved in dialogue, the next questions will be, "What'd I do, ref?" And, the answer is, "Oh, come on, I didn't do it." "Watch him for a change." While a partial running commentary may be suggested in some

"I didn't do anything, referee!" A loud whistle, intervention before the opponent retaliates, and sometimes words to the one who fouled... and get the game going. Picture is from the International Cup in Tokyo. In Japan, the crowds were quiet.

youth games, you do not need to justify or elaborate on your decisions for players over 16 years of age.

Remedy: Use your arm to signal direction of play, and move on. Keep the game moving. Almost every challenge to authority comes during a stoppage in play.

The faking of injuries.

Players who are injured do not roll over in pain. Their attention is solely on their injury, and they do not move or look around for decisions or support. Be aware of how players fall. Players, like some referees, are more fatigued just before the ending of a half.

Remedy: Caution for ungentlemanly conduct, but only if you are sure. Wait a moment, and see how a player "recovers" before deciding on a sanction.

"Diving" to the ground, usually in the Penalty Area.

Players who "dive" usually shout or grunt as they employ their rehearsed move.

Remedy: Stop play, caution the player for ungentlemanly conduct, and restart with an indirect free kick.

Arguing with Linesmen about offside decisions.

Players have a mistaken idea that Linesmen can be challenged independently of the referee. Let players know that you are a team. Instruct linesmen to report all dissent that you cannot hear.

Remedy: Immediately after offside or other decisions, move toward linesman, and get play started. "Good call", or "good flag", will show your support.

Defenders raising an arm for the referee's attention on an offside.

Even very experienced referees allow this to go on. Though players may be correct in their assessment of an opponent's position, the gesture is an unfair method of influencing a linesman or referee. This move is part of the offside trap plan for defenders, and must be discouraged.

Remedy: First time, warn the team. Second time, caution the offender.

TIME WITH THE CAPTAINS...
USUALLY THE BEGINNING
OF AUTHORITY

Every time a referee opens his mouth,
he opens up opportunities for players.

T here is a tradition in soccer for the coin toss meeting in the center of the field. The officials and the captains will meet, but it is not an excuse for dialogue. Each time an official presents his own well-chosen pieces of advice, often considered a threat to players, the integrity of all officials is being challenged. Respect the players as players. To gain the respect you wish, you must give it.

The formal pre-game at Guadalajara in the 1970 World Cup, England vs. Brazil. The captains each know which goal they want to defend the first half.

HINTS

- Captains are not to be reminded of their responsibilities and privileges. They already know them.

At the Dallas Cup, players always enter the field in disciplined fashion.

- Referees do not need to remind players of "10 yards", "playing the whistle", or about "forms of dissent". They already know.
- Players are not to be encouraged to ask questions on the Laws.

Too much talking can bring this response, even with young players.

- Your objective should be to create the most pleasant atmosphere on the field. This can be possible with a pleasant manner and with a firm handshake.
- Conduct your meeting 3 or 4 minutes before kickoff. This will allow last-minute instructions from the coach, yet not enough time for more warmups. Coaches, players and spectators should plan their time, knowing that the game will begin precisely on time.
- Any inspection of players' equipment must take place prior to the meeting with captains. Do this at least 15 minutes before kickoff, allowing for equipment change and for a brief warmup.
- If there are special conditions that are possible problems to your control or to the player safety, they may be briefly mentioned, with a request that the captain relay the information to the team. Examples of such conditions are:
  - the location of several fields close together (mistaken whistle or foreign objects such as another ball),
  - a cement track border close to the touchline, or
  - special field conditions that may not be evident due to overwatering or to raised sprinkler heads.

Everyone is smiles here at the Gothia Cup. It's a relaxed atmosphere. We all know it doesn't always end up that way!

CONTROL

"If you can keep your head when all about you
Are losing theirs and blaming it on you,
If you can trust yourself when all men doubt you,
You'll be a man, my son."

Rudyard Kipling

N o matter how good you think you are, or would like to be, you WILL make mistakes. You are NOT going to get every decision right. It is more realistic to want to achieve acceptance of all your decisions... that is game control.

If you believe in something, you should try to demonstrate that belief. BELIEVE in your every decision. Show it with a well-timed, energetic whistle, hand and arm signals that are influential and convincing, and with an authority that can be unquestioned. Remember that it is a normal tactic for players and coaches to test you early. Why should we be surprised that it happens?

Most players feel the need to be protected, to know that they can play without unfair interference. All players feel they can defeat the opponent. They feel they have better skills, conditioning, and preparation. When these players are careless or frustrated, they make borderline attempts at the ball. In the extreme, taking the ball away means taking the opponent out! Your task is to limit these fouls, and when they DO happen, discourage them from reappearing. That is game control.

Part of game control is displayed by USA FIFA referee, David Socha in an international game in Los Angeles. Here he has a bit of advice for goalkeeper Pat Jennings of Ireland.

Opportunity comes dressed in many forms. What should the linesmen be doing when the referee is attending to an injury stoppage?

Every referee has a bag of tricks called experience. Successful referees are flexible, knowing that they must "read" the game and decide which technique fits the occasion. Other referees repeatedly use the same technique, and seem surprised when it doesn't work. Abraham Klein once observed Johann Cruyff, the Dutch international, refusing to retreat 10 yards for a free kick. Klein knew what to do. The loudest possible whistle was blown less than two feet from Cruyff, startling him into action. Did it appear to be a deliberate move from Klein? Of course not! Just prior to the whistle, he appeared to be distracted from Cruyff. Later Cruyff said, "I've decided not to try to delay any more free kicks."

Solve one problem at a time on the field. Referees sometimes display the card before an incident has been diffused. Here is an excellent example of a problem that has not gone away.

You may have heard that it takes more muscles to frown than to smile, yet most referee smiles can be misinterpreted. Smiling is not a good technique, unless the laugh is on you. There is no one out there who's there to experience what you're experiencing, but everyone wants to experience what the players do! You have read elsewhere in this book that in intense international games you must have a firm grip on the game. Klein has a firm grip, then gradually releases it, allowing the advantage. If in every game you feel that "every foul must be punished", you are missing an opportunity described in Law V, International Board Decision 8.

Part of game control is controlling yourself. Do you find yourself joining the anger of the moment? Keep your head. Rarely display your anger. Use your great power with wisdom.

Two hours before a game, a FIFA referee checks out the measurement of the goal area. Though problems with the field could crop up at any time, this exercise is essential to game control. You can familiarize yourself, along with the linesmen, with general and specific field conditions as well as relaxing before the buildup of pre-game anxieties. Do you notice the goal line at the far post? It is wider than the post.

SOME HINTS FOR GAME CONTROL

1. First consider the "outer world" of your game. Are there problems from beyond the touchline? One problem from the bench near the touchline has more potential for disruption than 50,000 fanatics seated in the stands behind a barrier. Potential problems from bench and touchline activity must be immediately addressed.

2. Be aware of "flash points". The first minutes ("who is this opponent, and who is this referee?") and the last minutes (fatigue and unfulfilled expectations) of each period can be problems. The time following a goal (frustration and anxiety) can be further challenges to your game control.

3. When you first meet resistance, set the stage to meet that opposition. Stop play. Do not hurry. Deal with the problem by word and action. Deal with one problem at a time.

4. Consider writing a player's name on your game card WITHOUT an official sanction (red or yellow card). Doing this may prevent a reoccurrence!

5. Search for the "moment of truth" when problems can break out. It could be a seemingly unimportant incident, as two players contest for a ball that has passed over the touchline. Whistle, then the declaration of "red ball", "red throw-in", with the appropriate arm signal, should be a response.

6. Free kicks near goal can bring problems to the best of referees. Players, not referees, should decide whether the kick is "ceremonial". Referees, not players, should enforce the Law. Your firm, calm voice, the well-timed whistle, your location, and your signals will all tell a story: "The kick will happen, legally, and none shall interfere."

IT'S THE PLAYERS' GAME, EVERYONE'S LAWS, AND YOUR AUTHORITY!

What Others Are Saying...

"He's the world's #1 referee, and when Argentina's World Cup Champions played an All-World team down in Buenos Aires recently, FIFA assigned him to do the game."

Keith Walker, former NASL Director of Officials

WE LEARN FROM EACH OTHER

"The best team was the 'third team',
that of the officials."

Ken Aston

There is no substitute for objectivity from the touchline, particularly when it comes from Ken Aston, formerly Chairman of the Referee's Committee with FIFA. An interesting exchange took place during the time of a much publicized game during November 1976. England was playing Italy in a final qualifying match for the World Cup in Argentina, and the world knew that Klein would be the referee.

Aston considered the game "your qualifying match for 1978." With this prediction came, in Aston's carefully chosen words: "I think I should be less than enthusiastic about the use of Advantage, especially in the early stages."

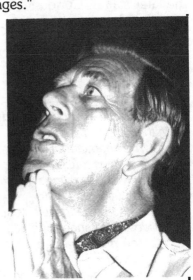

Ken Aston, creator of the red and yellow cards, is elated when they don't have to be used.

In preparation for the game, Klein spent much time viewing the film of the two teams, and was as prepared for the matchup as were the teams. Problems in the game were minimal, as Aston's wisdom was carefully acted upon. Aston later agreed that the tight control in the early stages protected the players and as fouls became less frequent, it was a safe and pleasurable game for all.

Following the game, and with full expectation that Klein would be on the FIFA list for Argentina, Aston offered help for a problem which has always plagued referees:

> **"Tighten up on the 10 yard distance at free kicks and watch encroachment before the ball is kicked rather more closely. I know it is a difficult situation for the referee, for he wants to get over the situation with as little trouble as possible. BUT IT IS A SITUATION WHICH IS A TRIAL OF STRENGTH AND DETERMINATION AND DISCIPLINE BETWEEN REFEREE AND PLAYERS AND EVERYONE PRESENT WANTS TO SEE WHO IS GOING TO WIN."**

In his final comments, Aston went on: "I was delighted to see that you did not use the Advantage in such a difficult match until the later stages. Curiously, it was then that you had to use the two yellow cards. I wonder if there is any connection between these two facts???"

When Not To Apply The Advantage
In the first ten minutes...
> *The character of the game has not been established.*

For a serious foul...
> *Players have good memories. The risk of retaliation is great.*

For a cautionable foul...
> *Authority needs to be established.*

Inside the defender's penalty area...
> *You must award a penalty, unless 99% sure of a goal being scored.*

When you have very young players (under "10")...
> *All players must understand fouls. This is a good time to learn.*

When you sense a loss of control...
> *There are many ways to slow the game down for the sake of control. This is one of them.*

10 REASONS FOR NOT WHISTLING A PENALTY KICK

1. When the players, coach, and spectators of the attacking team think you should.

2. When a player takes a dive.

3. When there was a penalty kick previously awarded to the other team.

4. When a foul is committed unintentionally.

5. When an indirect free kick should be awarded.

6. When players go down, but you're not sure what happened.

7. When you are not sure of the location of the foul.

8. When the linesman is not sure of the intention of the foul.

9. When you have decided to apply the advantage.

10. When you have decided that the ball was not in play.

It is possible that in spite of all the above reasons, you may not be calling enough penalty kicks. Consider the next page.

THERE IS ONLY ONE REASON FOR WHISTLING A PENALTY KICK...

If a penal foul is intentionally committed by the defense inside its own penalty area.

You must be in good position, confident of your decision, and be totally prepared to accept mild disapproval for your call. If there is dissent (continuing disapproval) through word or action, you must caution the offending player(s).

You may be whistling too many penalties, though there is only one reason to do so. Consider the previous page.

Everyone wants a penalty kick, except, of course, the defender in white.

What Others Are Saying...

"The pressure on Mr. Klein will probably exceed that of the players. He will have to strike a delicate balance between two opposing soccer cultures — the aggression, power, and courage of England, and the skill, cunning and emotion of Italy."

source unknown

MENTAL AND PHYSICAL PREPARATION

INTERNATIONAL SOCCER REFEREE
ABRAHAM KLEIN'S PERSPECTIVE

A referee who possesses good physical fitness does not get tired in the middle of a long run in the field. He arrives at high speed at the scene of action. This capability enables him to think clearly and to decide correctly. This is true especially towards the end of the game. A referee who is in good physical condition reaches the end of the game while he is still fresh and in possession of mental and physical abilities similar to those he had at the beginning.

Almost always at the end of games, critical moments occur in which the players commit fouls more frequently, either as a result of fatigue or because of a desire to use that last opportunity to change the result. A fresh referee will reach the scene of action immediately and will be able to control the game calmly.

The mental preparation of the referee should be started from the moment the referee gets his assignment (nomination to a game). He has to plan his schedule so that he will arrive at the field as early as possible. Those who come to the field at the last moment get into time pressure and this may result in having a negative influence on his decisions.

During one of the international games that I have observed, the referees arrived at the field at the last minute due to wrongly planning their time of departure from the hotel. The result was that they arrived at the game in a very distracted condition. They did not have enough time to brief and recheck as is necessary before a game, and a poor performance resulted.

What Others Are Saying...
"Klein was selected because of his strong resistance to intimidation."
Rob Hughes, International Herald Tribune

PERSONAL EXAMPLES FOR PHYSICAL AND MENTAL PREPARATION
from Abraham Klein's Rich Experience

A "In 1967, we were the referees in a tournament in Bangkok, Thailand. The temperature was about 104 degrees F. and the humidity was about 90%. A few monthsbefore this tournament, after rechecking the climatic conditions in Thailand, I trained for a long time in Israel, which has the same climatic conditions as Thailand. I had no physical problem coping during the game. I could easily function in the difficult climatic conditions."

B "I had the opportunity of being the referee in two important tournaments in Mexico. One was the Olympic Games in 1968 and the second was the World Cup Games in 1970. It is well known that Mexico City, and the other cities in Mexico in which the games took place, are located in extreme altitudes. The air is thin and therefore there is a lack of oxygen. This causes difficulties in long term physical activities. In order to overcome those problems or to get used to them, I planned all my training, a long time before the Olympic Games, in high places. And indeed as a result I passed all of FIFA's physical tests with high scores. The good results I achieved in those physical tests helped me to receive nominations to important games. The specific games' training program has to be prepared for the exact length of the game. It is also important to know if the games are in daylight or nighttime hours."

C Another example from Klein's experience for correct preparation comes from the final game of the 1978 World Cup. The games took place in Argentina in cold weather. "As I come from a hot climate, the change of weather from hot to cold was sharp and could have affected my physical fitness. So I planned my training in a country with a similar climate to Argentina, and when I reached there I did not suffer from any problems of adjustment."

D "An example of good physical preparation which affected my mental preparation directly occurred in the year 1972, one month before the Mini Cup Games, which were in Brazil. A short time before the games, I lacerated a muscle and I had my leg put in a cast. The doctors were convinced that I had to give up the idea of travelling to Brazil, but I did not give up. As a result of the great reserves which I had from the hard and continuous training before the injury, in addition to my determination which I consider to be my strongest characteristic, it became quite obvious that I would overcome the pitfall. I trained every day with the cast on my leg. I knew mentally that I could withstand the burden. Soon I gained my normal physical fitness, and in fact, I was assigned to referee six games at the tournament including the final match between Brazil and Portugal.

The conclusion from these examples is that there is a direct connection between physical and mental preparation. Without suitable preliminary preparations there is little chance that the referee will succeed.

It is most important for the soccer referee to be familiar with the teams he is going to meet. It is important to know preconditions, arrangements, the game venue, the condition of the field, the character of the crowd and whether or not the match will be coved by television. It is important to know the location of the teams in the league table, what the players' mentality is like, how those teams react to the behavior of the crowd.

All of these subjects are important. In order that the referee should be properly prepared, he has to think about planning his movements. He has to be concentrated and he has to arrive on the field at his best.

The referee has to be equipped with the proper tools to lead the game to full enjoyment, for the players, for the crowd and certainly for himself".

What Others Are Saying...

"As far as Klein is concerned, the 80,000 fans who howled and screamed at him and demanded unjustified penalties might just as well not been there. He ignored them. He built a wall of his own around the pitch."

source unknown

TRAINING PRINCIPLES

In order to properly use the training methods, we have to know and understand some "Training Principles". The "Training Principles" are the glue that joins the different parts of training into one unit.

1 **"The Progressive Loading Principle"**
This principle is used at two levels:
The first level is the training process. Training loads must be given moderately at the beginning of the season. The quantity is relatively low and the quality is moderate. Gradually, we increase the quantity and the quality.

The second level is the level of the training session. We start with a moderate warm-up and intensify the activity gradually.

First we have to increase the quantity.
Only after the body adapts itself to the load can we improve the quality.

---

2 **"The Principle of Optimal Relationship between Loading and Recovery"**. A specific training method will be effective for the referees only if the relationship between loading and recovery is kept. The table of "training methods" represents those relationships.

3 **"The Overloading Principle"**. The human body adjusts itself to physical loading. When such an adjustment occurs we have to increase the load in training until the body again adjusts itself. The referee should know when to increase the loading by executing some ability tests. Improving the results in those tests shows adjustment to the load. Increasing the load is also a matter of experience.

4 **"The Principle of the Proper Order of Stimulation Within the Training Session".** Much importance is attached to the content of the exercises and to the order in which they appear in one training session. If we are looking for good training effects, training Speed ability must always come before Endurancetraining.

This is because in Training Speed and Strength components, the trainee must always be fresh and not fatigued. If he proceeds with Endurance training before the Speed and Strength components, the trainee will probably be tired and there will not be Speed and Strength training effects. Training strength and speed can be simultaneously done only when the trainee doesn't activate the same muscles.

STRUCTURE OF THE TRAINING SESSION
- **Warm-ups:** easy jogging, breathing exercises, stretching, number of explosive strides with high knees on the spot. (7-10 minutes)
- **Flexibility training:** (10 minutes)
- **Speed training:** (7 minutes)
- **Strength training:** (7 minutes)
- **Endurance training:** (30 minutes)
- **Recovery:** (5 minutes)

This is a 70 minute training session. A training unit need not always include all the above elements.

---

5 **"The Principle of Variety".**
We have to vary the training sessions with methods and exercises. A person who is used to a certain method and similar exercises will not improve his ability.

6 **"The Principle of Training in Periods".**
A soccer referee faces 3 main periods:

First, a "Preparation Period" before the season. The referee must establish proper physical ability and prepare himself for the heavy load of the season. This period lasts two or more months.

4-5 training sessions a week is the minimum needed. A routine of 5 training sessions of 45 minutes is preferable to 4 training sessions of 60-70 minutes each!

Secondly, the In-Season Period. During this period the referee has to be at his best. He has to keep up his Endurance Ability and to sharpen, as much as possible, the Explosive Strength and Speed Ability.

A game and 3-4 training sessions per week is usually enough.

MOST IMPORTANT:
After the game, recovery by light jogging with stretching is highly recommended.

A MUST: Perform stretching and flexibility, followed by a hot bath, or, if possible, light swimming.

Thirdly, is the Transition Period: At the end of the season the referee goes into routine "Off Season". It is recommended that the vacation should not be a passive one. It is advisable to practice in any enjoyable physical activity which will make the body recover on one hand yet will not let him lose sharpness and gain weight.

7 **"Persistence principle"** - The soccer referee must be devoted in training. The moment he has decided on the number of training sessions per week, he has to fulfil it. He must not be distracted.

What Others Are Saying...

"Israeli referee Klein was made of sturdier stuff. He would not be intimidated when he refereed Argentina-Italy, not even when, at the start of the second half, a frenzy of whistling beat about his head from the steep terraces of the stadium."

Brian Glanville

COMPONENTS OF SOCCER REFEREE PHYSICAL FITNESS

WHAT IS PHYSICAL FITNESS?

Two definitions are accepted for "physical fitness". One is popular and is suitable for those who engage in recreational sports. The second definition is geared toward "elite-level" sport. Each of these areas defines its own meaning of "specific physical fitness".

DEFINITIONS

1 Physical fitness is the human being's ability to perform everyday activity in the best way, leaving energy reserves for unexpected events. Man's ability to perform physical tasks because of his profession or hobbies and at the same time leaving energy reserves for unexpected events, is "specific physical fitness".

2 Physical fitness is summing up all the factors of achievement in sports: The training state of the sportsman is expressed by the level of his physical and mental ability. Training physical fitness is training those skills.

The components of physical abilities and their importance and training varies from one activity to another. This is "specific physical fitness". In the introduction, we described the physical activities which the referee needs in order to control the soccer game. If we add specific activities to the effort, which is called "loading", it will be clear that the physical "loading" on the referee is from the first definition of "physical fitness". By adding the following variables:

- Clarity of thinking
- Keen marking after sharp whistle
- Firmness
- Leadership
- Crowd pressure
- Player pressure
- Ability to decide quickly

We will show that the second definition is the one that reflects the referee's physical fitness. Physical ability reflects the level of coordination and mental ability.

The parameters we have mentioned above must be at their best during the game, or failure is imminent.

GOOD PHYSICAL FITNESS REASSURES THE SOCCER REFEREE:

* Flowing movements: Both elegant and economic.

* Strong mental capacity throughout the game.

* Good coordination (ability) toward the end of the game

BASIC PHYSICAL ABILITY CHARACTERISTICS

DEFINITIONS AND TASKS

Physical ability consists of four components: **ENDURANCE, STRENGTH, SPEED and FLEXIBILITY.** These characteristics are independent of each other. However, a combination of two characteristics will give us other physical ability components:

Endurance + Strength = Strength Endurance

Endurance + Speed = Speed Endurance

Strength + Speed = Explosive Strength

Speed + Flexibility = Agility

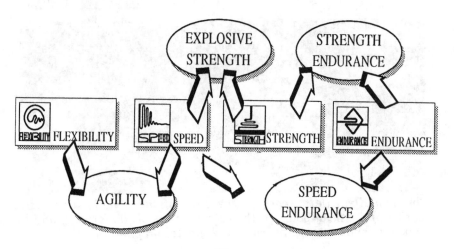

ENDURANCE

Endurance ability is expressed by continual long movements (over 8 minutes). High level endurance makes it possible for a referee to:

- Resist fatigue.
- Keep up the intensive efforts for extended periods.
  Recover quickly from physical efforts.
- **Endurance is the referee's most important physical characteristic.**

In addition to the above, endurance is a pre-condition for strength ability and for speed ability.

Endurance is connected to fuel supplies, or to the production of physical energy.

- The physical tools are: heart, blood vessels and lungs.
- Training endurance causes physical changes:
  - enlarging of the heart's muscle, thus creating increased stroke volume.
  - creating more blood vessels.
  - making blood vessels expand.
  - increasing the number of red blood cells and thus ensuring better oxygen transference.
  - better absorption of oxygen in the lungs.

Abraham Klein (left, rear), at the edge of the penalty area at the scoring of a crucial goal. To the referee, all goals are crucial, and the game demands intense physical and mental preparation.

STRENGTH

The referee's strength ability is the ability to overcome resistance and the ability to accelerate mass. His legs will carry him for 90 minutes at least - sometimes 120 minutes. His arms signal in a keen and clear way his instructions and commentary throughout the game.

- Strength - is expressed by muscle contraction. The muscle contraction is a chemical act that causes a mechanical act.
- Strength ability depends on the width of the muscle and its ability to activate "motor units".
- The physical tools are: skeleton and muscles.
- Training Strength causes physical changes:
  - Muscles thicken.
  - Increasing "glikogen" sources (energy material found in muscles and liver).

Training Strength ability is the basic pre-condition for explosive strength!

A soccer referee needs explosive strength many times during a game:

- A sudden burst of light running, or a short sprint, usually under thirty yards.
- To calm down a negative encounter.
- To enable close supervision of *any* event.
- To lengthen his strides and thus be much quicker.

All of the 1984 Los Angeles Olympics referees in an informal training session, under the watchful eye of a FIFA OFFICIAL. Friendly competitions among referees during these meetings is encouraged.

SPEED

Speed ability in sports is expressed by shortening the performance time. Speed is also expressed in the referee's ability to react immediately to different events in the game.

- The referee's ability to move from one place to another in a very short time is the outcome of superb nerve-muscle coordination.
- Speed ability is expressed by the most intensive movements one can produce over a time period of up to 8 seconds.
- The training of speed will cause:
  - Improvement of nerve-muscle coordination.
  - Quick reactions.
- Another basic pre-condition to improve explosive strength is the training of speed ability.
- Effective training of explosive strength and speed ability enables the referee to train properly for explosive strength ability.
- Speed training is the basic pre-condition to improve agility.

Superior conditioning will allow you to be on top of play at all times.

FLEXIBILITY

Flexibility means: better movement range of the joints.
- Tools: The active parts of the movement system: bones and cartilage.
- Flexibility training will enable:
  - better blood supply to all parts of the body.
  - prevention of injuries.
  - positive and quick recovery processes.
  - best movement range for the joints.
- Flexibility training is a basic pre-condition for improving agility.
- Good flexibility along with speed ability will give the referee appropriate agility. Agility in sport means: Sudden and quick direction changes.

Only #11 (on the ground) knows if there will be a problem following the foul. The whistle and the presence of Abraham Klein will limit the possibilities of a "blow-up". The endurance, speed, and strength of the referee all come into play here.

HOW TO TRAIN FOR
ENDURANCE

We have already seen the importance of the referee's endurance ability. Now we will deal with the methodical side.

How can we train for endurance? This section includes instructions for training examples and criteria for self examination and tests.

FIRST STEP: Exercises for adaptation of physical efforts.

At the beginning of the preparation period, the referee's physical condition will be at its lowest state. In order to improve his physical condition he has to train **gradually.** The first week of training will be more of a "scouting week" and a trial of coping with efforts.

- This training section is characterized by continuous loading but with low demands.
- Easy running which will be stopped from time to time by slow walking or stretching exercises.
- Fast walking, riding a bicycle and swimming in addition to other exercises.

SECOND STEP: Improving endurance by using training methods.

Adaptation to the kinds of effort written above is very fast. These efforts, when lasting a long time, do not improve a referee's physical ability and he will have to increase the training demands.

Means for checking:

- **Running distance:** it is advisable to reach 6-10 km run at this stage.
- **Running time:** running for less than 12 minutes is not considered effective in improving endurance. So, you have to aspire to a run that lasts about 30-45 minutes.
- **Percentage from the best performance:** after analyzing the different qualities of performance in the chapter about the "Training Methods", it was found that "continuous" jogging has has to be 60% of one's ability. In the "Extensive Interval Training Method" you have to run 60%-80% of your ability and in the "Intensive Interval Training Method" you have to run 80%-90% of your ability.

In this case the ability is the referee's highest performance for a certain running distance, which will be realized in training. For example: the referee's best performance for 400 meters is 1:00 minute. In order to run 70% of his ability, he has to add 30% of the time. That is 30% of 1:00 = 18 seconds. So the running time will be 1:00 min. + 18 sec = 1.18 min. This is a good and exact approach. Once a month, the referee must measure and estimate his ability in the different distances.

THIRD STEP: Loading evaluation by measuring pulse.

This approach is easy, convenient and exact. To measure pulse: Put your forefinger and middle finger on the inner part of your arm in line with the thumb on your wrist. You have

just found your pulse. After a physical effort, count the number of heart beats for 10 seconds only and multiply it by 6. Then you will get the number of heart beats per minute. It is not advisable to count heart beats for more than 10 seconds because the recovery process will cause the heartbeat to drop. If you cannot find the pulse in your wrist, put both fingers on your neck, between the esophagus and neck muscle. Repeat the counting as before.

HOW TO USE PULSE AS A LOADING REGULATOR

The referee has to know two important factors in order to use the pulse as a loading regulator: The pulse at rest and the maximal pulse possible.

Finding the pulse at rest: The pulse is to be measured in the morning when you wake up and before getting out of bed. Here, to be on the safe side, the heart beats have to be counted for 30 seconds and the result multiplied by 2.

Finding the maximal pulse: It is accepted that the maximal pulse of human beings at birth is 220 heart beats per minute. Every year of life, approximately one heart beat is lost from the maximal ability. A 30 year old man will have 200 heart beats per minute after a maximal effort. The ambitious referee is to execute maximal efforts at the beginning of the training period and measure the pulse for 10 seconds, multiplying by 6.

Maximal effort: Running "all-out" for 300 meters. Measuring the pulse must take place immediately after the run. It is best to ask for a partner's help. Those two values of the pulse will serve you along the way.

Here are a few examples for training according to the different periods and training methods:

Some given data:

John the referee is 30 years old.
Pulse at rest - 50 heart beats per minute.
Maximum pulse - 200 heart beats per minute.

a. John's pulse at the beginning of the preparation period: The following is a formula for finding the pulse in this period of training: The pulse in the "Continuous" method at the beginning of the training period = Rest pulse + 1/2 x (max. pulse minus rest pulse).

According to John's data:
$(50+1/2 \times (200-50))=50+75=125$.
According to this example, John had to reach a pulse of 125 per minute at the beginning of his training, which is 21 heart beats in 10 seconds.

b. John's pulse after adaptation to efforts: After a week or 10 days, John adapts himself to given efforts. At first he will run longer distances with the same pulse. (Increasing from 15 minutes to 25 minutes run). He will adapt to this as well. The next stage is to leave the running distance constant but to increase the intensity. Increasing intensity will be expressed by pulse raising. The following is the formula:

New pulse to be realized in training = Resting pulse + 2/3 x (max. pulse minus resting pulse).

ENDURANCE TRAINING

The resulting data:
50+2/3 (200-50)=50+100=150
According to this formula, after adapting to the previous efforts, referee John has to run at a rhythm that will bring his pulse to 150 heart beats per minute, which is 25 heart beats in 10 seconds.

c. **The pulse of referee John during "Extensive Interval" training:** The adaptation to "Continuous method" compels us to move on to the "Extensive Interval Training". At this level of training we would like to see the pulse increasing again, as the result of more intensive running. We multiply the difference between the maximum and resting pulses by 3/4 and add it to the resting pulse.

The new pulse realized in training:
50+3/4 (200-50)=50+112.5=162.5

d. **John's pulse during the "Intensive Interval" training:** The "Intensive Interval Training" is the highest level of training to improve endurance. The soccer referee does not necessarily need it, but if the training has begun on time, it is possible to integrate this method with others. According to previous examples, it is obvious that raising the quality of training will cause the pulse to be faster. We multiply the difference between the maximum and resting pulses by 4/5 and add it to the resting pulse.

ENDURANCE TRAINING

The new pulse:
50+4/5(200-50)=50+120=170
170 heart beats per minute which is 28 heart beats in 10 seconds.
These are examples only. The real training must take into consideration the individual differences.

Referee: In order to simulate exactly the endurance training you must know:
1. Your resting pulse
2. Your maximal pulse.

Examples for Endurance Training:

a. According to "Continuous" method:
- Continuous run for 30 minutes, 150 heartbeats per minute.
- Continuous run with geographic changes (ups and downs), sand, etc.
- Changing speed or speed-play for at least 30 minutes: 300m. easy jogging.
  + 30m. sprint + 200m. easy jogging
  + 300m. tempo running + 300m. easy jogging + 30m. sprint.

b. According to "Extensive Interval" training:
8 x 2 minutes running, 70%, 1 minute pause.
500m. 80%, 1 minute rest.
2 x (200m. + 300m. + 400m. + 500m.
   + 400m. + 300m. + 200m.) x 2.
1 minute rest after each distance.

c. According to "Intensive Interval" method:
 - 8 x 150m. 90% - 1:30 min. rest.
 - (50m. + 100m. + 150m. + 200m. + 150m.
     + 100m. + 50m.) x 4 at a strong tempo.
 - Resting until the pulse goes down to 120 heart beats.
 - 60-100m. uphill running - 8-10 repetitions (or 15-20 secs.) - resting till pulse of 120.

Dr. Kenneth Cooper, the sports expert and founder of the Cooper Aerobic Fitness Center in Dallas, Texas, stated the above criteria for Endurance ability.

The figures below provide estimates of endurance ability as a function of age. The distance, in meters, are for a 12-minute run.

Men:

Ability Estimation	Up to 30 years	30 - 39	40 - 49	Over 50
Very good	2800	2650	2500	2400
Good	2400	2250	2100	2000
Fair	2000	1850	1650	1600
Weak	1600	1550	1350	1300

Women:

Ability Estimation	Up to 30 years	30 - 39	40 - 49	Over 50
Very good	2600	2500	2300	2150
Good	2150	2000	1850	1650
Fair	1850	1650	1500	1350
Weak	1550	1350	1200	1050

ENDURANCE TRAINING

All numbers are meters.

HOW TO TRAIN FOR
STRENGTH

The referee's most important muscles which have to be strengthened are the muscles that guard the spinal cord: stomach, back, chest and buttocks. Long distance and continual jogging, sometimes in high intensity, require an early preparation for those muscles. Their task is to stabilize the upper body. A referee who does not pay attention to this important point endangers himself in the long run, and may suffer from severe backaches.

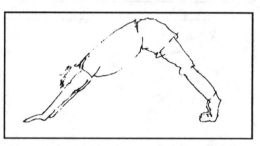

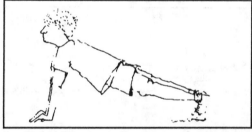

Maximal push-ups in different positions. Maximal sit-ups at different angles.

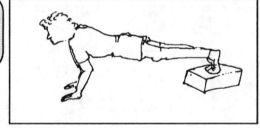

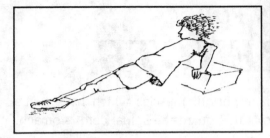

The legs' capability for explosive strength has to be trained constantly.

ARMS AND HANDS STRENGTH

- Push-ups:
  - hands on a higher place,
    body horizontal.
  - working with dumbbell or medicine ball.

ABDOMINAL MUSCLES

- Sit-ups:
  - hands behind neck, legs lifted and crossed.
  - similar position - right elbow across left knee, left elbow across right knee
- Body leaning on the forearms , lifting the feet 7 inches from the ground and crossing them.

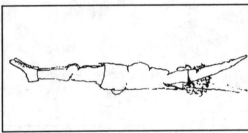

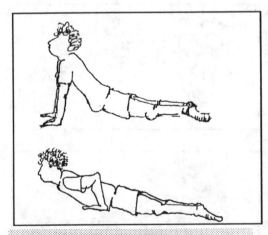

Note: The isometric exercise has to be repeated 5-6 times with 15 to 20 seconds rest.

- Isometric abdomen - 45 degree sitting position while the hands are kept behind the back for 10 seconds.
- Isometric abdomen - body leaning on the forearms with legs stretched for 10 seconds.
- Hyper extension of the back - hands on the sides for 10 seconds.
- Hyper extension of the back - hands straight forward for 10 seconds.
- Hyper extension of the back, hands in each one of the above movements for 10 seconds. (illustration on page 72)

Isometric exercise: An exercise "pitting" one muscle against another or against an immoveable object, such as pushing two hands together or pushing down on a desk.

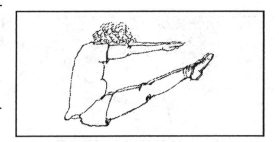

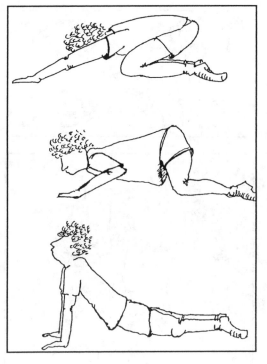

IMPROVING EXPLOSIVE STRENGTH IN THE LEGS

- Different jumps: high jumps, jumps with knees bent and squat jumps.
- Running up stairs.
- Jumping on one leg. Switching legs. Jumping on both legs.
- Side jumps. 5m. sprints.
- Squats with weight on the shoulders.

For your convenience - illustrated examples are included on how to improve strength ability.

HOW TO TRAIN FOR
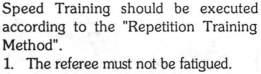
SPEED

Speed Training should be executed according to the "Repetition Training Method".

1. The referee must not be fatigued.
2. The training should be after suitable warmups.
3. The exercises should always be executed with highest speed possible.
4. Between exercises, always have a full rest until you feel recovered.
5. Once you get tired and the quality of performance is reduced, stop the high-speed exercising!
6. 600 m. easy jogging and additional stretching after speed exercises.

SPEED TRAINING EXAMPLES

- 10 x 10m. - sprint, from normal standing position.
- 6 x 20m. - sprint, position as mentioned above.
- 3 x 50m. - sprint, position as mentioned above.
- A few sprints down hill.
- Short sprints, changing starting positions.
- Sprints around obstacles.
- Sprints while changing direction.

HOW TO TRAIN FOR
FLEXIBILITY

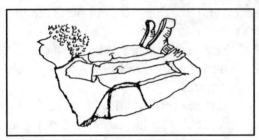

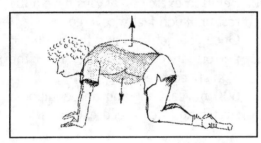

The referee must be flexible in the ankles, the knees, the groin, the back and the shoulders. Flexibility can be developed in two ways:

1. Dynamic flexibility. The referee moves the joint he is interested in making flexible.
2. Static flexibility. The referee puts pressure on the joint he wants to make flexible until mild pain is evident. When this occurs he should continue pressing for 10 seconds more, then repeating this exercise for more flexibility.

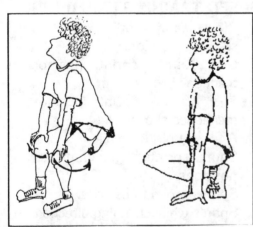

On the following page are illustrations showing the most important flexibility exercises for referees.

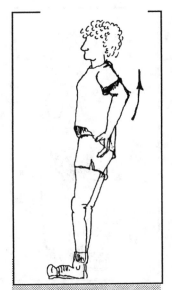

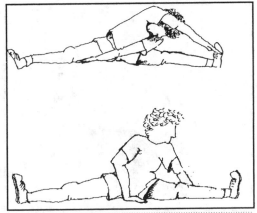

FLEXIBILITY

REFEREE! TRAIN CORRECTLY, AND USE TRAINING METHODS WISELY.

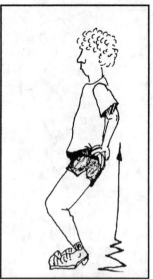

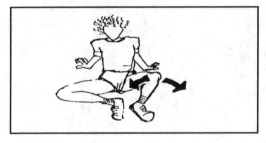

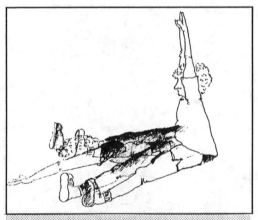

TRAIN REGULARLY!

PROGRAM EXAMPLES
EXAMPLE 1

The following represents a typical week's training beginning 2 months before and until 2 weeks before the season.

FOR ONE WEEK'S
TRAINING

FIRST TRAINING:

- 7 minutes warm-up including easy jogging and stretching.
- 15 sit-ups to the front, 15 sit-ups to the right, then left and relax.
- 2 x 15 hyper-extensions of the back - hands to the sides.
- 20 minutes jogging (pulse according to the given formula).
- Relaxing and stretching.

Training time - about 45 minutes.

> It might be difficult for the referee to run 20 minutes intensively. Our advice is to run until you get tired, then keep on walking while relaxing and recovering. Continue running after a few minutes. Once you finish running, you must relax and perform stretching exercises.

SECOND TRAINING:

- 12 minutes free warm-up exercises including jogging and stretching.
- 5 x 20 m. sprints at highest speed. Full recovery.
- Relaxing and stretching. Strengthening exercises as in the first training session. Relaxation.
- 20 minutes light jogging (pulse as in given formula).
- Relaxing and stretching.

Training time - about 60 minutes.

> The refereee who is still not capable of running 20 full minutes, will see that fatigue begins to affect his running much later. After running, you must relax and perform stretching exercises.

THIRD TRAINING:

- 7 minutes warm-up exercises.
- Strengthening exercises from the previous trainings.
- 20-30 push-ups. Relaxation.
- 20 minutes light running.
- Relaxing and stretching.

Training time - about 45 minutes.

PROGRAM EXAMPLES

EXAMPLE 2

2 WEEKS Before the
SEASON

FIRST TRAINING:
- 12 minutes warm-up exercises.
- 6 x 15m. sprints at high speed.
  Full recovery. Relaxing and stretching.
- 8 x 400m. - running at leisurely pace. (according to
  the formula: multiply the resting pulse and maximal pulse
  by 3/4 and add 50. Rest until pulse goes back to 20 heart
  beats in 10 seconds.) Relaxing and stretching.
- 1500m. light run.
- Flexibility.

Training time - about 60 minutes.

> During this period of training try to execute the
> strengthening exercises in the morning. Research shows
> morning training is more efficient.

SECOND TRAINING:
(As an example for the referee who could not practice strengthening exercises in the morning)
- 7 minutes warm-up exercises.
- 7 minutes of practicing bounces for feet strengthening.
  (choose exercises from the "strength" chapter).
- 25 sit-ups to the front.   25 sit-ups to the right.
- 25 sit-ups to the left. Relaxation
- 2 x 30 hyperextensions of the back. Relaxation.
- 2000 m. of continual running within speedplays.
  Change directions, run backwards, run with crossed legs.
  Finish the run with a pulse close to maximal!
  Relaxation and flexibility.

Training time - about 45 minutes.

THIRD TRAINING: Repeat the first training of this week.
FOURTH TRAINING: If you have enough time - it is worth-
while to repeat the second training of this week!

PROGRAM EXAMPLES

EXAMPLE 3

A week of training at mid-season.

FOR ONE WEEK
IN SEASON

FIRST TRAINING:

After the game you have to execute a recovery training.
Possibilities:

- 2000m. light jogging in addition to stretching and flexibility exercises.
- Long and enjoyable swim, in addition to relaxation exercises in the water for the leg muscles.
- Enjoyable "flat surface" ride on a bike (about 30 minutes) in addition to stretching and flexibility exercises.

Training time - about 35 minutes.

SECOND TRAINING:

- 12 minutes warm-up exercises.
- Stretching and relaxation. Chosen strength exercises.
- 5x300m. according to the "extensive interval method" - in moderate tempo in order to conserve endurance.
- 2500 m. - speed play running.
- Relaxation.

Training time - about 45 minutes.

THIRD TRAINING:

- 12 minutes warm-up exercises.
- Stretching and flexibility
- 8x10m. speed training, full recovery.
  - 100 - 200 - 300 - 400 - 500 - 400 - 300 - 200 - 100 - short rest between distances. Moderate tempo.
- 2500 m. speed-play running.
- Relaxation.

Training time - about 60 minutes.

If the referee's physical fitness is good, it is recommended that he should perform one recovery training session and another 2-3 training sessions per week.

PHYSICAL FITNESS TRAINING METHODS

We have discussed the referee's physical demands, by defining "physical fitness" and physical ability components.

Now we'll deal with the training methods. The training methods enable us to train for physical fitness. Each training method must be based on the following variables:

Distance - (when running is considered).

Number of **sets.**

Intensity.

Number of **repetitions.**

Rests between repetitions and sets.

THE COMMON TRAINING METHODS

1 **"The Continuous Method":**
This method is executed by continuous movements, with no interruptions, and recovery only at the end of the activity. The quality of performance is moderate or low, and the tempo does not change.

The goals of this method are:
- Endurance improvement - especially at the beginning of the training season.
- Recovery from efforts - by light jogging for a few minutes.

2 **"The Speed-play Method":**
This method is similar, in practice, to #1. The difference is in the method of executing the practice. The "Speed-play" method gives the opportunity to use fast movements along with slower ones. After establishing a stable aerobic level by using the first method, you can begin using The Speed-play Method. (After approximately after two to three weeks of training.)

3 **"The Extensive Interval Training Method":**
In this method the trainee repeats a certain distance (400-100m.) with significant repetitions (6-15). The velocity is moderate to sub-maximal (60%-80%) of the maximal personal ability. The recovery between repetitions is not fully gained. The new start will be when the pulse goes down to 120 heart beats per minute. Count the heart beats for 10 seconds and multiply by 6.
- **The goals of Extensive Interval Training Method:**
  - Improving endurance.
  - Maintenance of endurance ability. During the season when the referee is at the top of his physical capability, maintenance of endurance will be achieved by performing exercises on a level of 60% of his ability and 60% of the former training volume.

Due to the rest between repetitions, the quality of performance can be higher than the quality in the Continuous Method. This method has to be performed after achieving a good level of endurance using the first two methods.

4 **"The Intensive Interval Training Method":**
This training method is similar to the previous in its construction. The difference is in the performance quality. The velocity of the performance is 80%-90% of the maximal ability. As a result, the distances covered in training will be much shorter (100-400m.). The number of repetitions is less (5-10). The recovery between repetitions lasts until the pulse goes down to 120 heart beats per minute. The Intensive Interval Training Method is the most qualitative method to improve endurance and therefore, the most difficult. It is to be used only after achieving basic endurance ability in the other methods and after 6 weeks training.

5 "The Repetition Training Method".

The Repetition Training Method is characterized by short distances (up to 50m.) and short time (2-8 seconds) performance. In this method, the number of repetitions is small (5-8) and recovery between repetitions is fully gained. Full recovery means the ability to repeat the distance at high speed. (100% of the actual ability). In the Repetition Training Method the intensity is at its highest.

- **Goals of "Repetition Training Method":**
  - Speed ability training
  - Training the nerve-muscle coordination. - Fast reaction ability training.

The following table concludes the training methods and gives some training examples.

Training Method	Volume	Intensity	Recovery	Exercise examples
"Continuous Training Speed-play"	Long to very long up to 12 km. running and up to 45 min. uninterrupted activity	Low to moderate	Only after activity	• 4000 m. of continuous running, even tempo at 60% of the best performance • 4000m. run - built up as follows: 300m. light jogging + 100m. sprint + 200m. light jogging + 50m. sprint + 300m. jogging and so on.
"Extensive Interval Training"	Long up to very long	Medium to sub-maximal	Short, pulse back to 120 heartbeats per minute	• 8 x 400m. - 80% 1-2 minutes rest • 6 x 600m. - 70% 1-2 minutes rest
"Intensive Interval Training"	Medium	Sub-maximal 80%-90%	Until pulse goes back to 120 heartbeats per minute	• 10 x 100m. - 90% 2-3 minutes rest • 6 x 300m. - 85% 2-3 minutes rest
"Repetition Training"	Very short	Maximal 100%	Full, until the ability to repeat the high performance	• 8 x 10m. - 100% • 6 x 20m. - 100% • 4 x 30m. - 100%

MENTAL STRESS

A Part of Life, A Part of Refereeing

T he pressures on the referee far exceed that of the players. The crowds, the media and a tense atmosphere for players brings problems for those who are not mentally prepared. Decisions may pacify or inflame temperaments. Even correct decisions are not always accepted.

Moderate stress can be healthy. You must, however, find ways of coping with extreme stress. Acute stress decreases the referee's ability to meet the challenges of decision making. Mild stress begins the moment the referee is aware of the assignment, could increase, but must be controlled.

The body produces certain hormones in times of high stress. Though the hormones' presence may diminish stress, they can produce harmful side effects if produced for long periods of time. Response to stress is individual. No two body chemistries or mental capacities are the same.

Each event requires us to adapt. The need to adapt to new situations is a form of stress. The pressure to make literally thousands of decisions in a match can produce great stress for any referee. Unless we find methods of unburdening ourselves from game and other forms of stress, our health could be threatened.

A few common, yet serious, results from undue stress are:

- High blood pressure
- Heart attacks
- Ulcers
- Headaches
- Back and neck aches
- Inflamed joints
- Sleeplessness
- General poor health due to weakness or immune system deficiencies

Stress can affect general behavior in the following ways:

- Listlessness
- Overindulgence in unhealthy activities, such as eating and drinking
- Feelings of tension and depression

A SOLUTION
A training program for Muscular Relaxation

Abraham Klein has successfully dealt with problems of mental stress. A most effective solution lies in a simple training program for muscle relaxation. This causes the pulse to decrease, lowering the blood pressure. This enhanced blood flow throughout the body brings on mental relaxation as well.

The program requires an even surface for lying down. Here you can better concentrate, even simulate an actual game and the demands that will come your way.

A foul at midfield, a player down, and a teammate takes the law into his own hands. The referee is pointing off the field, signifying a "sending off", yet the problem is not solved. Note a teammate of #15 in the background, sprinting to his teammate's defense.

1   Put your hands at your side, and relax. Close your eyes and take a slow, deep breath into your stomach. Filter the air slowly between your teeth, and exhale. Repeat three times.

2   Feel your body sink heavily into the surface on which you are lying. Scan your body in your imagination - from the feet through the tips of your fingers - relax and "sink" into the surface.

3   Make a tight fist of your right hand. Hold for ten seconds. Open the fist, and stretch out your hand as much as possible. Think about how it feels. Feel warm, pleasant, and relaxed. Repeat three times.

4   Repeat the procedure with your left hand.

5   Repeat the deep breathing exercise. (Step #1)

6   Close your eyes tightly and let your face muscles tighten as hard as possible. Hold this position 10 seconds. Feel the warmth expand through your face and then release your muscles slowly. Repeat this action 3 times.

7   Repeat the deep breathing exercise.

8   Clench your teeth, concentrate on your jaw. After a few seconds release the clenched jaw slowly. Repeat this action 3 times.

9   Inhale, again, deep into your stomach. Wait a few seconds and exhale the air slowly.

10 Contract your shoulders until you feel tension on the upper shoulder, the back part of the neck and the side of the neck. Wait a few seconds for the warm feeling and release your muscle slowly. Repeat the action 3 times.

11 Repeat the deep breathing process.

12 Make your stomach muscles contract deeply. Concentrate on how you feel and release the muscles slowly. Repeat this action 3 times.

13 Repeat the deep breathing exercise.

14 Make your legs contract very tightly. Concentrate on the "tightening" sensation. Try to increase the intensity of contraction. Release the muscles slowly. Repeat the action 3 times.

15 Repeat the deep breathing exercise.

16 Breathe normally. Scan again, in your imagination, your body. You are relaxed, sunk on the surface on which you lie, all loosened. While mentally scanning your body, release the muscles which remain in an unrelaxed state. Imagine the tension leaving the body. Lie in this position for a few minutes.

17 While having a pleasant feeling of losing everyday worries, concentrate on your task on the field. Try to recall the most exciting experiences you have ever had in your career as a referee. Think of those experiences which have bolstered your self confidence and given you confidence that you would like to repeat. Feel that you are recharging power and that there is nothing in the world that can prevent you from doing your job in the best possible way.

18 After a few minutes, begin "to come back to life". Your eyes are still closed. Begin to move the tip of your toes. Prepare your body for essential activity. Now shake your feet and ankles. Gently strike the surface on which you are lying with your feet. Move your shoulders, and hands. Turn your head slightly. Feel your awakening.

19 While your eyes are still closed, inhale as much as you can, into your chest this time. You should feel as if you are filled with power which you did not have before. When filled with air, wait a few seconds, filter the air slowly out, between your teeth. Repeat the chest breathing 3 times.

20 Now you are strong, relaxed, full of motivation for the coming events. Open your eyes. Arise slowly and gently to maximize the experience.

A stressful situation for both players and referee. There is no doubt here that #5 was fouled, and #20 is saying, "Come on, it was nothing." Referee Klein is aware of the problem, with a whistle, and an immediate card, coming from the right breast pocket. While sometimes the foul cannot be prevented, the response to the foul can be.

ADDITIONAL INSTRUCTIONS

- Mental relaxation technique can be repeated and made a daily routine.
- The more you increase your skill in performing the technique, the shorter the process.
- In the beginning, the technique will take about 20 minutes. But in time, the relaxation technique can be accomplished in about 10 minutes.
- Gentle, soft background music is advised to further blot out distractions.

Are You Ready For This?

A free kick was awarded to the attacking team, 20 yards from goal. Two attackers stood on either side of the ball, apparently discussing who would take the kick. Seizing the opportunity to organize a defense while the attackers "argued", the goalkeeper moved toward one post. A third attacker quickly ran between the two teammates and shot the ball into the unprotected side of the goal. All of the defense had been caught flat-footed, and they protested a "quick kick", but a brilliant ruse had worked to perfection. This tactic presupposed a referee who would not impose himself unnecessarily into a nonceremonial kick situation.

Note: The game referee, in an unprofessional yet understandable reaction to this creative tactic, and in thanks for the lesson he learned in NOT interfering with play, offered his game fee to the coach of the team who took the free kick. Understandably, it was refused!

Are You Ready For This?

A travelling university team from Mexico specialized, it seemed, in an offside trap that constantly left attacking forwards in an offside position. With a precision that almost defies description, defenders would quickly sprint forward just enough to cause the offside position, yet with a margin that would eliminate any doubt. When balls were played forward, attackers were called offside by at least two meters. Now, more than 20 years later, the referee in that game still vividly recalls an ultimate tactic as a further safeguard. The goalkeeper, playing well in advance of his penalty area, would also quickly move to intercept passes when the "trap" was sprung. Usually as the whistle blew, the goalkeeper would comfortably and confidently have the ball at his feet!

PRACTICAL NUTRITION

A Vital Link to Top Performance

U sing the method of the "Five Food Groups" is an effective method for achieving balanced nutrition. This plan will be discussed here for general health, followed by specific recommendations for the special needs of athletic training for the referee.

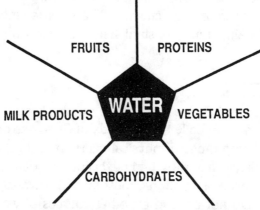

This is a combined nutrition approach to health, applicable to vegetarians and meat-consuming persons alike. It is recommended that the following components should be included in the daily menu.

CARBOHYDRATES - 10-15 portions daily

PROTEINS - 2 portions daily (low fat content)

FRUITS - 2-6 portions daily

VEGETABLES - 4-6 portions daily

MILK & MILK PRODUCTS - 3 portions daily

WATER - That special need which must not be forgotten.

*A minimum of 8 glasses daily.

Proteins are needed by the body to build and rebuild cell tissue. It is recommended that proteins should supply 10% of the needed daily intake requirements for optimum nutrition. A referee's correct daily menu does not demand additional protein. Too much can be harmful to the body.

Fats are necessary in the daily intake, and should come primarily from vegetable sources, decreasing the amount of fats from meats. It is recommended that fats in the diet should not exceed 20% of the daily nutritional intake. Deep-fried foods and high-fat milk products are to be avoided.

A balanced menu and correct eating habits should supply adequately all of the vitamin and mineral needs required for the normal physical activities of the referee.

Following these guidelines for healthy nutritional living should produce the opportunities for maximum enjoyment and efficiency for refereeing activities. The referee strives to be a true athlete by maintaining constant habits of good nutrition, exercise and rest.

WATER

The number one need of the physically active person is cool water. The normal daily bodily needs of 8 glasses of water must be increased during times of physical exertion. Often, in hot weather, the loss of liquid from the body exceeds one quart, and this liquid must be replaced. The referee must take his own supply of water to the game.. Do not depend on other sources of water -- take your own.

Plain water is the very best liquid for refreshing the body and replacing fluids for body tissues. It is _not_ recommended to drink carbonated beverages, sugared drinks, or, obviously, alcoholic drinks. Drinks in which the sugar content is more than 5% are not recommended for any sportsman. Even fruit juices are not good just before, after, or during physical activity, due to their high sugar content. Milk and milk-drinks are high in protein, so are not recommended. Those drinks or food products which contain sugars or proteins, food components which need to be digested, are not desirable, since one's energy must be directed to the activity itself rather than to digestion.

Immediately before the game, the referee should drink one cup of water. During half-time, your own water supply should be available, and then an increased amount of water after the game. Lack of water replacement can cause headaches, dizziness, increased body temperature, yellow urine and apathetic behavior.
DRINK, DRINK, DRINK!!

CARBOHYDRATES

10-15 portions daily - one portion equals:
1 Slice Bread
1/2 Cup Cooked Rice
1 Potato
1/2 Cup Pasta
1 Banana
1/2 Cup Corn
1/2 Cup Legumes (beans)
2 Crackers - whole wheat
1/2 Cup Cornflakes
1/2 Cup Green Peas

PROTEINS

2 portions - 100 grams (before cooking) daily.
Beef
Poultry - turkey, chicken
Liver
Fish
Soy Beans and its products
Legumes & Nuts (raw)
1 egg
1/2 Cup Cottage Cheese
Yellow Cheese - 1 slice

FRUITS

2-4 portions daily to include one portion of citrus fruit. One portion equals:

1 Orange	1 Peach
1/2 Grapefruit	2-3 Apricots
1 Cup Grapes	1/2 Melon
1 Banana	1 Slice Watermelon
1 Pear	1/2 Cup Dried Fruit
1 Apple	1 Cup Fresh Juice
2-3 Plums	

VEGETABLES

2-4 portions daily. One portion equals:

 1 Tomato
 1 Cucumber
 1 Green Pepper
 1 Onion
 1/4 Eggplant
 1 Squash
 3 Leaves Lettuce
 1/2 Cup Broccoli, Cauliflower, Cabbage
 1 Cup Peas or Beans (green or yellow)

MILK & MILK PRODUCTS

2-3 portions daily. One portion equals:
 1 Cup Milk
 1 Cup Yogurt
 1 Cup Cocoa
 1/2 Cup Ice Cream - low fat
 1/2 Cup Cottage Cheese
 1 Slice Yellow Cheese

These are the main components and proportions needed for normal nutritional health. This is a "balanced diet". During times of increased physical activity, adjustments must be made for the increased energy needs. During training periods the referee will need 500 to 1500 calories more than he needs during inactive times. The additional energy requirements depend upon the amount and intensity of the training, taking into account climatic conditions.

The energy sources from food are of special interest to the referee. Carbohydrates are the main "fuel" for strenuous muscle work. It is recommended that 60-70% of the soccer referee's nutrition comes from carbohydrates. This is a special source for maintaining muscle strength, endurance and energy.

Patterns of general nutrition, health and well being must be ongoing for a dedicated soccer referee. The referee must be a true athlete, maintaining constant habits of good nutrition, regular exercise and rest.

For optimum health, energy, and overall efficiency, a high-carbohydrate, low-fat, high-fiber diet is recommended. During periods of hard training the referee should eat more carbohydrates for the additional energy needed by the body during exercise. The more complex carbohydrates (potatoes, fruit, vegetables, salads, pastas, rice, grains) consumed during periods of exercise, the more energy is available for the muscles to use. Proteins, fats and sugars should be avoided during periods of training (meat, cheese, peanut butter, eggs, milk, oils).

Nutrition Before Games

Eat a meal rich in carbohydrates the evening before the game and three to four hours before the game. *Avoid eating a heavy meal before a game.* Avoid eating fats and proteins. You must come to a game with all of the energy your body can produce, available for the physical and mental efforts of the assignment.

Italy-Argentina, 1978. It was the only game Argentina lost enroute to its first World Cup Championship. The physical and mental preparation for a match like this must be thorough, impeccable. There is no room for a mistake. Note the decision near goal, with a loud whistle and simultaneous signal.

THE UNIVERSAL EXPERIENCE

It happens to every referee, early in the career. First there's a foul, some minor dissent, then a retaliation foul. Then words on both sides, some from players who weren't even involved. Players soon lose concentration on the ball, fearing still another foul, and protect themselves by the raised knee or the foot over the ball. The ball becomes secondary and players will soon deal with ithe referee's loss of control on their own terms. The words are ugly, and the big explosion isn't far away. Several players may be sent off and the game will not reach an acceptable conclusion.

In his initial year as a referee in Israel's First Division, Abraham Klein analyzed his own performance in a game that ended early: "It was my fault. It was bad refereeing. I vowed it would never happen again."

Here's what he decided:

- Firmness must begin with the referee's first contact with players. This may even be in the dressing room.
- Be closest to play in the early stages. Do not apply the advantage.
- Allow no dissent that can be heard by others.
- Whenever possible, communicate with the player who is fouled, as well as with the guilty one. This can sometimes be done with simple eye contact.

There is no substitute for being close to play.

UEFA INSPECTOR

A braham Klein has recently been appointed to Inspector of Games for UEFA (Union European Football Association). Assignments are made by UEFA on a game-to-game basis for all international competitions under their jurisdiction. An Inspector's task is twofold: (1) To work with the team officials to determine that the highest standard of preparation is evident in both the stadium and in the "behind the scenes" facilities. (2) To assess the performance of referees and linesmen.

Included in the Technical Instructions to Officials are both the principles of refereeing and the observations on the Laws of the Game. These reminders highlight areas which have led to problems in the past, and are similar to that of those given to World Cup referees. Some interesting points are summarized here:

Basic Principles of Refereeing UEFA Matches

Deliberate offenses committed with the intention of harming or intimidating an opponent usually trigger off more unpleasant scenes, and must be severely punished. Particular attention should be paid to holding, kicking, punching, and pushing.

Try to take up positions which will give you a good side view of goalmouth incidents.

It is important to work together well with linesmen, but it is always the referee who makes the decisions.

Observations on the Laws of the Game

If a player who is to be substituted refuses to leave the field of play, there is no reason for the referee to intervene. This is a matter for the team captain or team officials.

To avoid doubt on any incident, make notes during the game. Ask one linesman to make notes as well.

Referees and linesmen who have been appointed to a UEFA game, should wherever possible, officiate together in at least one match of their own domestic league before the UEFA match itself.

The referee should look towards his linesman whenever a goal is scored.

Under no circumstances should the linesman signal if he merely feels or thinks that an offense has been committed.

Any player who deliberately delays the restart of a match or leaves the field of play to celebrate the scoring of a goal must be cautioned.

The referee alone is responsible for judging whether a player in an offside position is actually affecting the play.

A goalkeeper who prevents an obvious goal scoring opportunity by stopping the ball with his hand or hands outside the penalty area shall be sent off.

Offenses committed in the penalty area must not be dealt with differently than those committed in midfield or elsewhere on the pitch.

If a goalkeeper moves his feet too early and if no goal is scored, the penalty kick has to be retaken.

Attention should be paid to ensure that the ball is thrown in more quickly and do not give the opportunity for any bad sportsmanship through time wasting.

Lennart Johanssan is the President of U.E.F.A.

REFEREES AND THE FUTURE

Measuring Physical Field Performance

W hat distance does a referee travel in a 90 minute game? Estimates vary, between 4-8 miles. The jogging, sprinting, walking, side-stepping, and backward movements add up to continuous action under physical and mental stress. We know that at game's end the referee should be as capable as at the opening whistle.

The modern referee has new friends, Zvi Friedman and Jonathan Kotas. Their "Second Look" for soccer became an instant success at the 1994 World Cup. This unique software product was utilized by the coaches of both the U.S. and Brazil national teams. "Second Look" is a graphic representation of key match events, and can track all activities in a game.

Now, SOFTSPORT is developing, under the supervision of Abraham Klein, a referee performance analysis kit for referees and linesmen. "Individual officials can benefit greatly from this product. Instantly they will be able to visualize, then analyze their physical field performance," says Friedman, who is an active coach, formerly National Head Coach for the American Youth Soccer Organization, and an advisor to the U.S. National Team.

Referees are invited to contact SOFTSPORT at (818) 887-4259 or fax them at (818) 887-4210.

Zvi Freedman (right), and Jonathan Kotas at the Rose Bowl in Pasadena, California, at halftime during the Final.

FROM GENERATION UNTO GENERATION...

Amit Klein, 32, is an urban geographer, and has been officiating for almost half of his young life. His ascent to the FIFA list began in Haifa, when he was 17. The youth leagues and adult leagues first saw his service to soccer. With both parents as physical educators and with vivid memories of his dad in the NASL, Olympics, and World Cups, Amit had a chance to think long and hard about the physical and mental preparation that would be required. Just eight years ago, he became the youngest referee in the Israel First Division League, a good training ground for the rigors of international play.

Amit, who served for four years in Special Rescue for the Army, received his FIFA badge in January 1995, and now serves as one of Israel's three referees on the elite FIFA list.

TRAINING WITH AMIT KLEIN

Duration:	One hour daily.
Sunday:	Long jogging on the beach - 8000 m.
Monday:	Sprint series - 10m. to 100m. (running forward, backward, sidestep running) total: 2500m.
Tuesday:	Series of intervals - 100m. - 600m.
Wednesday:	Series of intervals - 1000m. Each less than 4 minutes.
Thursday:	Repeat of Monday's training.
Friday:	Rest.

All training begins with warming up and stretching, and ends with stretching.

Saturday:	Match day. Light breakfast, leisurely 30 minute walk. Mental preparation by reviewing information on teams, relaxing in bath.

ADVICE FROM A FORMER FIFA REFEREE
TO HIS SON, AMIT, A NEW FIFA REFEREE

1. Refereeing is not the most important thing in your life. Your family, education, job, and friends are of more value.
2. Love refereeing, and enjoy each minute. It's a "hobby" for you, but remember that playing is a profession to some.
3. Be an example to other referees, and learn from everyone.
4. Your mistakes can be excused, but don't make the same mistake twice.
5. Referee in your own way. Don't try to emulate others.
6. Organize your own life. Be disciplined and live like an athlete.
7. Expect to work very hard.
8. Be honest, and humble.
9. Be strong mentally and physically.
10. Prepare yourself for every game.

Amit Klein (center) with his two Israeli linesmen in Cyprus, February 1995. The Norway-Cyprus "friendly" was his first FIFA assignment as a referee.

With Franz Beckenhauer of Germany. Beckenhauer captained his team in World Cup competition and later coached the national side.

With Jack Warner from Trinidad and Tobago. Jack is President of CONCACAF (Confederacion Norte-Centroamericana y del Caribe de Futbol).

WOMEN REFEREES
ON THE WORLD SCENE

In January 1995, FIFA announced their first Provisional List of Referees and Lineswomen. Twenty-five women from twenty-two countries have been listed as FIFA referees. Twenty-nine women from twenty-one countries are FIFA lineswomen.

Denmark and Brazil each have the honor of having placed two nominees on each list. The Danish officials on the FIFA list:

REFEREES

Bente Folsing
has officiated 627 games

Gitte Nielsen
has officiated 347 games

LINESWOMEN

Gitte Holm
has officiated 84 games

Lotte Walde
has officiated 168 games

Refs' problems are same world over

ON REFEREES

Klein looks tough enoug~

Klein a must for Argentina

The high acclaim which Abraham Klein, the 42-year-old Israeli referee, received from all quarters for his firm handling of the vital Italy-England World Cup tie in Rome last week should make him a certainty for the finals in Argentina in 1978.

Among the 80,000 spectators at the match was FIFA president, Joao Havelange, who had particularly warm praise for Klein's performance.

In the welter of words which have been written about the match the British press was unanimous in their admiration of the referee.

The "Daily Mail" picked him out as being the one man responsible for the game failing to become the bloody battle everyone had predicted it would be: "Referee Klein . . . deserved the pay of princes for his command of these warring kings" and "It was tough, it was uncompromising, it was honestly refereed."

HUNGARY'S manager Lajos Baroti is in no doubt— "If the referees do not do their job in Argentina, it will be the death of football."

With at least half a dozen teams committed unashamedly to tactics of intimidation, the role of the referees has never been more important, writes David Miller.

Abraham he knows all about trouble

Abraham restores our faith

THE first authentic hero of the 1978 World Cup has emerged at last—and it is not a pampered, overpaid professional footballer.

WELL DONE, MR. KLEIN

To the Editor of The Jerusalem Post

Sir, — Full marks to Mr. A. Klein, the Israeli referee of the World Cup match between England and Brazil on June 7. Like many thousands of other TV viewers in the United Kingdom, I was most impressed by his very intelligent and efficient handling of this match which undoubtedly took place in a highly charged atmosphere. The enjoyment of a continually flowing great match was in no small measure due to Mr. Klein's skill: Well done, Sir!   R. H, ELDER
Highcliffe, England, June 8.

Klein Dirigirá la Final?

REFEREES THROUGH HISTORY

WHO WILL REFEREE WORLD CUP '98?

METERS TO YARDS
CONVERSION TABLE

METERS	YARDS	METERS	YARDS
5	5 + 1'	1350	1476
10	10 + 2'	1500	1640
15	16 + 1'	1600	1749
20	21 + 2'	1650	1804
30	32 + 2'	1850	2023
50	54 + 2'	2000	2187
100	109	2100	2296
150	164	2150	2351
200	218	2250	2460
300	328	2300	2515
400	437	2400	2624
500	546	2500	2734
600	656	2600	2843
1050	1148	2650	2898
1200	1312	2800	3062
1300	1421		